FOOD
in a flash!

Over 60 quick recipes low in Points

Roz Denny

SIMON & SCHUSTER
A VIACOM COMPANY

First published in Great Britain by Simon & Schuster UK Ltd, 2003. A Viacom Company.

Copyright © 2003, Weight Watchers International, Inc.

Simon & Schuster UK Ltd.
Africa House
64–78 Kingsway
London WC2B 6AH

Weight Watchers and Time to Eat are Trademarks of Weight Watchers International, Inc. and used under its control by Weight Watchers (UK) Ltd.

Photography: Iain Bagwell
Styling: Rachel Jukes
Food preparation: Penny Stephens
Design: Jane Humphrey
Typesetting: Stylize Digital Artwork
Printed and bound in Hong Kong

Weight Watchers Publications Manager: Corrina Griffin
Weight Watchers Publications Executives: Lucy Davidson and Mandy Spittle

A CIP catalogue record for this book is available from the British Library.

ISBN 0 74323 136 8

Pictured on the cover: Thai Prawn and Pepper Stir Fry, page 17
Pictured on the back cover: Fruits of the Forest Cream, page 50
Pictured on the title page: Spicy Fish Burgers, page 27

Raw eggs: Only the freshest eggs should be used. Pregnant women, the elderly and children should avoid recipes with eggs which are raw or not fully cooked.

Recipe notes: Egg size is medium unless otherwise stated. Fruit and vegetables are medium size unless otherwise stated.

Recipe timings are approximate and meant to be guidelines. The preparation time includes all the steps up to and following the main cooking time(s).

 You'll find this easy to read Points logo on every recipe throughout this book. The logo represents the number of Points per serving each recipe contains. The easy to use Points system is designed to help you eat what you want, when you want – as long as you stay within your Points allowance – giving you the freedom to enjoy the food *you* love.

V This symbol denotes a vegetarian recipe and assumes that free-range eggs and vegetarian cheese are used. Virtually fat-free fromage frais and low-fat crème fraîche may contain traces of gelatine so they are not always vegetarian. Please check the labels.

Vg This symbol denotes a vegan dish.

contents

healthy meals in
30 minutes
or less

Do you ever feel that you are missing out on wholesome, nutritious meals, simply because you don't have the time to prepare them? Then this book is ideal for you! Life today is becoming increasingly busy and many people find themselves short of time – making it all too easy to grab a processed meal that is high in Points but low in nourishment. Eating freshly cooked food that is well balanced and healthy is an important part of staying in control of your weight. With *Food in a Flash!*, you can forget all your time worries, as all the recipes take 30 minutes or less from start to finish, and are low in Points – perfect if you are following the Weight Watchers Time to Eat Programme.

Many families are finding it more and more difficult to sit down and eat together. Meal times are the perfect opportunity to share news and views with your loved ones. The *Family Meals* chapter in this book gives you a wonderful selection of family dishes, with something for every occasion, and no one will ever guess that it is 'diet' food! And, as all the recipes are so quick to make, you'll get more time to enjoy the company of your friends and family!

From filling soups and starters to wonderful puddings and bakes, no matter what you're looking for, we are sure you'll find a fabulous low Point treat. Check out the *Meals for One or Two* chapter, and see how easy it is to rustle up something tasty and nutritious just for you, with little time and effort. And as the recipes are all Pointed for you, you can rest assured that they will easily fit in with your Time to Eat Programme. There's also an entire chapter dedicated to filling and tasty vegetarian dishes and lots more vegetarian alternatives throughout the book.

All the recipes have been created with you in mind! Preparation and cooking times have been cut to a minimum, with the flavours and satisfaction levels pushed to the maximum. So go on – tantalise your taste buds and cook up some Food in a Flash!

Celery and
Tomato Soup:
fill up on the
lovely, fresh
flavours for
zero Points.

starters

& soups

Take the edge off your hunger pangs with one of these light and healthy dishes. It can be all too easy to tuck into high Point foods just because they are easily accessible. So this section contains a good range of quick and easy snacking foods like patés and simple salads, as well as more substantial soups and warm starters. Soups can also double as light main meals and are fantastic if you are watching your weight because they leave you feeling very satisfied without using up too many valuable Points.

CELERY AND TOMATO SOUP

0 Points per recipe

Ⓥ (Ⓥᴇ) *Serves: 4*

Preparation time: 10 minutes

Cooking time: 20 minutes

Calories per serving: 45

Freezing: recommended

The popular combination of celery and tomato is wonderful in this zero Point soup. It's a tasty and clever way to deal with those hungry moments – without adding extra Points.

---

4 celery sticks, chopped finely

1 onion, chopped finely

1 carrot, grated coarsely

1 large garlic clove, chopped

low fat cooking spray

420 g can of chopped tomatoes

500 ml (18 fl oz) vegetable stock

salt and freshly ground black pepper

To garnish

1–2 tablespoons chopped fresh parsley

a few small celery leaves

---

1 Place the celery, onion, carrot and garlic in a large saucepan and spray them with low fat cooking spray. Heat until the vegetables sizzle and then add 6 tablespoons of water.

2 Cover and cook gently for 10 minutes, shaking the pan occasionally. Stir in the chopped tomatoes and then the stock.

3 Add some seasoning and bring the pan to the boil. Reduce the heat and simmer for another 10 minutes, or until the celery is tender. Check the seasoning. Ladle the soup into four bowls and sprinkle with chopped parsley and the small celery leaves. Serve hot.

Variation You can turn this into a spicy Mexican style soup by substituting a chopped green pepper for the celery and adding ½–1 tablespoon mild ground chilli and ¼ teaspoon ground cumin in step 1. The Points will stay the same.

Delicious, creamy Mushroom Paté is the perfect start to any meal for just 2 Points per serving.

MUSHROOM PATE

8 Points per recipe

Ⓥ *Serves: 4*

Preparation time: 10 minutes

Cooking time: 15 minutes

Calories per serving: 120

Freezing: not recommended

This rich tasting mushroom paté is served with melba toast and makes an elegant starter or lunchtime treat. A salad of mixed green leaves makes a good accompaniment.

---

250 g (9 oz) button mushrooms, ideally chestnut mushrooms

1 tablespoon low fat spread

1 large garlic clove, crushed

½ teaspoon dried thyme

1 tablespoon light soy sauce

200 g (7 oz) quark

2 tablespoons finely chopped chives or green tops of spring onions

salt and freshly ground black pepper

For the melba toast

4 medium slices of brown or white bread

---

1 Set aside two mushrooms for a garnish and then finely chop the remainder. You can do this in a food processor.

2 Melt the low fat spread in a large saucepan and lightly sauté the garlic for about 1 minute. Stir in the mushrooms, and then add 6 tablespoons of water, the thyme and seasoning.

3 Heat the mixture until it starts sizzling. Cover the pan and cook gently for about 10–12 minutes, shaking the pan occasionally and stirring once or twice, quickly returning the cover to the pan. The mushrooms should soften in their own steam.

4 Meanwhile, make the melba toast. Preheat the oven to Gas Mark 3/160°C/fan oven 140°C. Lightly toast the bread slices. Remove the crusts and then carefully cut through the soft centre of each toast to make two very thin slices. Now cut each thin slice diagonally to make 4 triangles and place them on a baking sheet. Bake them in the oven until the edges curl. Remove the toasts and cool them until crisp.

5 Cool the mushrooms and stir in the soy sauce and quark until you have a smooth and creamy mixture. Mix in the chives or spring onion tops. If you prefer a smooth paté then purée everything in a food processor.

6 Spoon the paté mixture into a medium size bowl or divide it between four ramekin dishes. Slice the reserved mushrooms and arrange the slices on top. Chill in a refrigerator to make the texture firm.

SMOKED HADDOCK AND CORN CHOWDER

 2 POINTS

9 Points per recipe

Serves: 4

Preparation time: 10 minutes

Cooking time: 20 minutes

Calories per serving: 200

Freezing: recommended

A delicious main meal soup that is fish, potatoes and corn all in one. Serve this with two cream crackers per serving, adding 1 Point per portion.

200 g (7 oz) potatoes, peeled and chopped finely

4 spring onions, chopped

2 teaspoons low fat spread

½ teaspoon mild curry powder (optional)

300 ml (½ pint) skimmed milk

300 ml (½ pint) fish, vegetable or chicken stock

300 g (10½ oz) smoked haddock

170 g can of sweetcorn, drained and the liquid reserved

salt and freshly ground black pepper

1 tablespoon chopped fresh parsley, to serve

1 Put the potatoes, spring onions, low fat spread and curry powder, if using, into a large saucepan with 4 tablespoons of water. Heat until the mixture is sizzling, and then cover and simmer for 10 minutes, shaking the pan occasionally. Do not let the ingredients burn.

2 Remove the cover, stir in the milk and stock, and bring to the boil. Reduce the heat and simmer for 5 minutes.

3 Meanwhile, skin the fish. Slide a sharp, straight bladed knife between the flesh and the skin of the fish, and work in a sawing motion to remove all the skin. With your fingertips, check the flesh for any pin bones and pull them out.

4 Chop the fish into small cubes and add them to the simmering pan along with the sweetcorn and the reserved liquid. Gently boil the soup and cook for 5 more minutes, until all the ingredients are tender. Check the seasoning and serve, sprinkled with the parsley, in four warmed bowls.

Top tip Curry powder has zero Points, so it's always best to use it rather than curry pastes which have a high oil content.

Variation If you love the sound of a creamy chowder, but aren't too keen on fish, try using 2 × 100 g (3½ oz) skinless chicken breasts instead of the haddock. Chop the chicken breasts into 1 cm (½ inch) cubes and add them at step 2 with the milk and stock. The Points per serving will be 2½.

Smoked Haddock and Corn Chowder: a wonderfully filling and delicious soup. Accompanied by two cream crackers it's only 3 Points per serving.

BACON AND SPINACH SALAD

4½ Points per recipe
Serves: 2
Preparation time: 15 minutes
Cooking time: 15 minutes
Calories per serving: 110
Freezing: not recommended

Take a bag of baby spinach leaves and turn them into a quick, warm salad for a light lunch or starter. The wonderfully crunchy croûtons here are a low fat version of the variety you find in supermarkets and are much more delicious.

200 g pack of baby spinach leaves
1 medium slice of wholemeal or brown bread, crusts removed
low fat cooking spray
a pinch of dried oregano or thyme
50 g (1¾ oz) lean back bacon, diced finely
1 tablespoon balsamic vinegar
1 spring onion, sliced into long, thin strips
2 good pinches of sesame seeds
salt and freshly ground black pepper

1 Wash the spinach leaves, if necessary, and dry them thoroughly. Place the leaves in a bowl, cover and set aside.
2 Heat the oven to Gas Mark 6/ 200°C/ fan oven 180°C. Spray the bread slice evenly on both sides with the low fat cooking spray and then cut it into small squares. Arrange the squares in a single layer on a baking sheet, season and sprinkle them with the herbs. Bake them for 15 minutes until they are lightly crisp. Remove the baking sheet from the oven and allow the croûtons to cool – when they will become even crispier.
3 Heat a non stick frying pan until you can feel a good heat rising, and then spray it with low fat cooking spray. Sauté the bacon, stirring, until it is lightly browned. Stir in the balsamic vinegar and immediately add the spinach and spring onion, tossing it all to make sure the spinach leaves are well coated with the vinegar.
4 Check the seasoning and divide the mixture between two plates. Sprinkle over the sesame seeds and top with the croûtons before serving.

Top tip You can make a large batch of croûtons and store them in an airtight container to use at another time.

CHUNKY CHICKEN MINESTRONE

5 Points per recipe
Serves: 4
Preparation time: 10 minutes
Cooking time: 20 minutes
Calories per serving: 130
Freezing: recommended

This is a delicious and filling main meal soup. Make lots of this soup and then freeze what you don't eat for a quick snack when you are feeling hungry.

1.5 litres (2¾ pints) boiling water
2 chicken stock cubes
2 × 100 g (3½ oz) skinless, boneless chicken breasts
1 leek, sliced thinly
1 carrot, grated coarsely
a good pinch of dried mixed herbs or dried thyme
2 tablespoons quick cook macaroni or small soup pasta shapes
1 small courgette, chopped
3 tablespoons garden peas
1 sprig of fresh basil, torn (optional)
salt and freshly ground black pepper

1 Pour the boiling water into a large saucepan and crumble in the stock cubes and bring to the boil. Stir until the stock cubes are dissolved.
2 Now, carefully add the chicken breasts, leek, carrot, dried herbs and seasoning. Simmer for 15 minutes until the chicken is cooked.
3 Remove the chicken breasts with a slotted spoon. Now stir the pasta, courgette and peas into the pan. Simmer for a further 5 minutes.
4 Meanwhile, cut the chicken into small cubes. Return the chicken to the soup and check the seasoning. Stir in the basil, if using, and serve the soup hot in four warmed bowls.

Variations Leave out the macaroni and the soup will be 1 Point per serving.

You can also vary the vegetables according to the season or to suit your tastes.

If you substitute 2 tablespoons of basmati rice for the pasta, the Points per serving will remain the same. Add the rice to the soup in step 3. Simmer for 10 minutes.

CHILLI BEAN SALAD

8½ Points per recipe

Serves: 2
Preparation time: 20 minutes
Calories per serving: 270
Freezing: not recommended

Kidney beans can form a great basis for a fast and filling salad or light meal. This delicious salad tastes superb served with rye crispbread – remember to add the extra Points.

2 rashers lean back bacon
200 g can of red kidney beans, drained and rinsed
1 celery stick, sliced thinly
2 spring onions, chopped
1 carrot, grated coarsely
1 medium tomato, chopped
2 tablespoons fat free French dressing
a few drops of hot pepper sauce (e.g. Tabasco)
4–6 large lettuce leaves
40 g (1½ oz) half fat Cheddar, cut into small cubes
1 punnet of mustard cress
salt and freshly ground black pepper

1 Grill the bacon rashers for about 3–4 minutes until they are crispy. Cool and then chop them finely. Set aside.

2 Place the kidney beans in a large mixing bowl. Stir in the celery, spring onions, carrot and tomato. Add the dressing, hot pepper sauce, chopped bacon and seasoning.

3 Line two shallow bowls with the lettuce leaves and divide the bean salad between the bowls.

4 Scatter the cheese and mustard cress over the salad. Serve it immediately, or lightly chill it in the refrigerator.

Variation Try a 170 g can of sweetcorn and 100 g (3½ oz) whole green beans, blanched, instead of the kidney beans. The Points per serving will be 3½.

ZERO POINT STUFFED PEPPERS

0 Points per recipe

Ⓥ Ⓥᵉ *Serves: 2*
Preparation time: 10 minutes
Cooking time: 15 minutes
Calories per serving: 70
Freezing: not recommended

For a wonderful, tasty treat, it's hard to beat these halved peppers filled with colourful vegetables. Serve them warm for a zero Point starter.

1 red pepper
1 yellow pepper
1 medium courgette, sliced thinly
low fat cooking spray
8 cherry tomatoes, halved
2 good pinches of dried oregano
salt and freshly ground black pepper

1 Halve the peppers lengthways and remove the seeds and membranes. Trim the stalks but do not pull them off.

2 Heat the oven to Gas Mark 7/ 220°C/fan oven 200°C. Bring a large saucepan of water to the boil, add the courgette slices and blanch them for 1 minute. Drain them well and spray them with low fat cooking spray, carefully tossing them to coat the slices. Season to taste.

3 Place the courgette slices in the pepper halves. Lay the tomatoes on top of the courgettes, cut side up. Season again and sprinkle over the herbs.

4 Bake for 15 minutes, until the peppers and tomatoes start to soften. Allow them to cool slightly before serving.

Zero Point Stuffed Peppers. Vegetables have never tasted so good!

CURRIED LENTIL SOUP

3½ Points per recipe

Ⓥ Ⓥᵍ Serves: 4
Preparation time: 10 minutes
Cooking time: 20 minutes
Calories per serving: 105
Freezing: recommended

Split red lentils are cheap, very quick to cook and high in no fat fibre and protein. They're used here in this wonderful warming soup that is lovely and filling, but uses few Points.

low fat cooking spray

1 medium onion, chopped

1 large garlic clove, chopped

1 small green pepper, de-seeded and chopped finely

1 large fresh green chilli, de-seeded and chopped finely (optional)

1 teaspoon mild curry powder

75 g (2¾ oz) dried split red lentils

200 g can of chopped tomatoes

1 litre (1¾ pints) vegetable or chicken stock

salt and freshly ground black pepper

1 tablespoon chopped fresh coriander or parsley, to serve (optional)

1 Heat a large saucepan and spray it with low fat cooking spray. Add the onion, garlic, pepper, chilli (if using) and 4 tablespoons of water to the pan. Heat until it all starts to sizzle. Stir, cover the pan and simmer for 5 minutes, stirring once half way through.

2 Add the curry powder and cook for 1 minute and then stir in the lentils, tomatoes, stock and seasoning.

3 Bring the pan to the boil, and then reduce the heat and simmer for 12–15 minutes, until the lentils

thicken and soften. Check the seasoning and serve in large bowls sprinkled with chopped coriander or parsley, if desired.

Top tip If you just want a hint of chilli, then don't cut it up – add it whole at step 2 and remove before serving.

ITALIAN RICE AND PEA SOUP

13 Points per recipe

Serves: 2
Preparation time: 5 minutes
Cooking time: 25 minutes
Calories per serving: 380
Freezing: not recommended

If you like filling, comfort food then try this classic Italian country soup. It makes the ideal all in one meal.

low fat cooking spray

1 small onion, chopped

2 rashers lean back bacon, trimmed and chopped

100 g (3½ oz) risotto rice

3 tablespoons white wine (optional)

750 ml (1⅓ pint) boiling chicken or vegetable stock

125 g (4½ oz) frozen peas

25 g (1 oz) Parmesan cheese, grated

salt and freshly ground black pepper

1 Heat a large saucepan and spray it with low fat cooking spray. Add the onion, bacon and 2 tablespoons of water to the pan, and cook until the mixture sizzles. Cover the pan and cook on a medium heat for 5 minutes until the bacon and onion have softened.

2 Stir in the rice and cook for 1 minute. Add the wine, if using, and cook until it has evaporated.

3 Add the stock and seasoning, and bring the mixture to the boil. Reduce the heat and simmer for about 15 minutes, stirring occasionally, until the rice is tender and the soup has thickened. It should have the consistency of runny porridge.

4 Add the peas and cook for another 3 minutes. Stir in half the cheese. Serve immediately, sprinkled with the remaining cheese.

Top tip When cooking with alcohol always boil it for a good 1–2 minutes. This ensures that the flavour is less harsh.

Variation You can use 125 g (4½ oz) frozen sweetcorn instead of the peas and 4 spring onions instead of the ordinary one. The Points per serving remain the same.

For just 1 Point per serving, this Curried Lentil Soup is so easy to prepare and it tastes so good!

Leek and Mushroom Gratin: a creamy dish of soft, savoury vegetables with a crunchy, cheesy topping. 2 Points per serving.

LEEK AND MUSHROOM GRATIN

4½ Points per recipe

Ⓥ *Serves: 2*

Preparation time: 10 minutes

Cooking time: 15 minutes

Calories per serving: 100

Freezing: not recommended

A fantastic starter that tastes wonderfully indulgent, without using too many Points.

---

low fat cooking spray

1 large leek, sliced thinly

125 g (4½ oz) mushrooms, sliced thinly

1 large garlic clove, chopped

1 tablespoon light soy sauce

2 tablespoons single cream

1 tablespoon chopped fresh parsley

1 tablespoon Parmesan cheese, grated

1 tablespoon dried natural coloured breadcrumbs

salt and freshly ground black pepper

---

1 Heat a large saucepan and spray it with low fat cooking spray. Add the leek, mushrooms and garlic with 4 tablespoons of water and cook until the mixture sizzles. Cover and cook on a medium heat for 10 minutes, shaking the pan occasionally, until the vegetables have softened.

2 Add the soy sauce and seasoning, and then mix in the cream and the parsley.

3 Preheat the grill. Divide the leek and mushroom mixture between two ramekin dishes. Mix together the Parmesan cheese and breadcrumbs and then scatter this over the leek and mushrooms.

4 Place the dishes under the preheated grill, until the tops are crisp and golden brown. Cool slightly and serve.

SWEET AND SOUR CAULIFLOWER SALAD

1½ Points per recipe

Ⓥ Ⓥg *Serves: 2*

Preparation and cooking time: 20 minutes

Calories per serving: 95

Freezing: not recommended

This is an unusual and tasty way to serve cauliflower. The sweet and sour dressing is delicious tossed with any crunchy zero Point vegetables.

---

1 small cauliflower

1 small red onion, sliced thinly

1 small courgette, cut in medium cubes

½ yellow pepper, sliced finely

1 tablespoon chopped fresh parsley

salt and freshly ground black pepper

For the dressing

2 tablespoons light soy sauce

2 tablespoons white wine vinegar

1 tablespoon dry sherry (optional)

2 teaspoons clear honey

1 teaspoon sesame oil

4 tablespoons boiling water

---

1 Halve the cauliflower. Then remove the thick stalk and discard. Cut off the florets and trim their stalks right down. Bring a large saucepan of lightly salted water to the boil. Add the cauliflower florets, onion and courgette, and blanch them for 2–3 minutes until they are tender, yet still crisp.

2 Drain the vegetables well and tip them into a mixing bowl. Whisk the dressing ingredients together and stir it into the cooling vegetables.

3 Add the pepper and parsley. Season and serve warm.

Variation Add 25 g (1 oz) of thinly sliced cold ham. The Points per serving remain the same.

SPICY STIR FRIED PRAWNS

3½ Points per recipe

Serves: 4

Preparation and cooking time: 15 minutes

Calories per serving: 75

Freezing: not recommended

Prawns teamed with crunchy mange tout or sugar snap peas make a winning combination. This stir fry makes a simple and satisfying starter.

---

200 g (7 oz) mange tout peas or sugar snap peas

1 large fresh red chilli, de-seeded and sliced thinly

1 large garlic clove, chopped

low fat cooking spray

200 g (7 oz) frozen peeled prawns, defrosted

1 teaspoon ground cumin

1 teaspoon ground coriander

½ teaspoon ground ginger

1 tablespoon soy sauce or Thai fish sauce

2 tablespoons chopped fresh coriander or parsley

juice of 1 lime

salt and freshly ground black pepper

---

1 Place the mange tout peas or sugar snap peas, chilli and garlic in a frying pan and spray them with the low fat cooking spray. Heat until sizzling and then add 3 tablespoons of water. Cook, stirring, for about 3 minutes until the vegetables have softened.

2 Mix in the prawns and spices, and stir fry for 2 minutes. Add the soy sauce or fish sauce, ground black pepper, herbs and lime juice. Check the seasoning and serve.

Enjoy this Thai Prawn and Pepper Stir Fry for just 2½ Points per serving. It's just as delicious as a take away but much lower in Points.

meals
for one or two

Most people lead busy lives, and often it is not possible to sit down for a meal with friends and family, so a range of dishes for one or two people is ideally suited to today's lifestyle. All these recipes are perfect for those who come in from work hungry or are in a rush, with ingredients that can be picked up in a small supermarket. If you choose a recipe for two but need it for one, then either halve the ingredients or save half for the next day.

THAI PRAWN AND PEPPER STIR FRY

2½ POINTS

2½ Points per recipe

Serves: 1

Preparation time: 10 minutes

Cooking time: 15 minutes

Calories per serving: 210

Freezing: not recommended

This is a very quick and easy stir fry using peeled prawns and colourful vegetables.

---

low fat cooking spray

½ small red pepper, de-seeded and sliced thinly

1 shallot, or ½ small onion, sliced thinly

1 large garlic clove, crushed

50 g (1¾ oz) mange tout or sugar snap peas

1 tablespoon light soy sauce

1 teaspoon dry sherry

¼ teaspoon sesame oil

a pinch of sugar

125 g (4½ oz) peeled prawns, defrosted if frozen

a dash of hot pepper sauce (optional)

a pinch of sesame seeds

---

1 Heat a wok or a large non stick frying pan until you can feel a good heat rising and spray it with low fat cooking spray. Add the pepper, shallot or onion, garlic and 2 tablespoons of water. Stir fry over a medium heat for 3 minutes until the vegetables have softened.

2 Stir in the mange tout or sugar snap peas and cook for another 2 minutes, until they have wilted.

3 In a cup, mix together the soy sauce, sherry, sesame oil and sugar with 1 tablespoon of water. Add this to the pan, stirring well.

4 Now, mix in the prawns and heat through until it is all piping hot. Add the pepper sauce, if desired, and serve sprinkled with sesame seeds.

Variations For an extra special treat use shelled and deveined tiger prawns.

Cook 60 g (2 oz) of noodles or long grain rice per serving to accompany this dish for a filling meal. Add 3 Points per serving.

Top tip Sesame oil is a brilliant addition to Chinese and Thai dishes. It's very aromatic and adds lots of flavour. Don't cook with it however as it burns very easily.

This is a delicious, well balanced and healthy dish – wonderful as a satisfying and tasty evening meal.

300 g (10½ oz) baby new potatoes, scrubbed

low fat cooking spray

1 onion, chopped

1 large garlic clove, crushed

1 teaspoon ginger purée (optional)

1–2 teaspoons mild or medium curry powder

4 tablespoons canned chick peas, drained

2 teaspoons plain white flour

150 g tub of very low fat natural bio yogurt

200 g pack of baby spinach

salt and freshly ground black pepper

fat cooking spray. Add the onion, garlic, ginger purée (if using) and 4 tablespoons of water and cook until the mixture sizzles, and then cover and reduce the heat. Cook for 5 minutes until the onion has softened.

3 Add the curry powder, to taste, the sliced potatoes and chick peas to the pan. Cook for 1 minute. Stir the flour into the yogurt and add this to the pan. Heat gently until the sauce thickens.

4 Now, gradually stir in the spinach leaves, until they have all wilted and are thoroughly mixed in. There is no need to precook the spinach, as the leaves are so tender. Check the seasoning and serve the curry piping hot in two shallow bowls.

This Spinach and Chick Pea Curry is great for a mid week supper – it's tasty, quick and just 3 Points per serving.

SPINACH AND CHICK PEA CURRY

 3 POINTS

6½ Points per recipe

Ⓥ Serves: 2

Preparation time: 12 minutes

Cooking time: 15 minutes

Calories per serving: 245

Freezing: recommended

1 Cook the potatoes in lightly salted, boiling water for about 12 minutes, until just tender. Drain, cool and cut them in thick, even slices.

2 Meanwhile, heat a medium size saucepan and spray it with low

CREAMY CRAB LINGUINE

5 POINTS

9½ Points per recipe

Serves: 2

Preparation time: 5 minutes

Cooking time: 15 minutes

Calories per serving: 320

Freezing: not recommended

Dressed crab is available in most supermarkets and it works wonderfully in this simple and delicious seafood sauce for pasta.

75 g (2¾ oz) linguine or tagliatelle

170 g can of sweetcorn, drained

1–2 spring onions, chopped

43 g can of dressed crab

2 tablespoons half fat crème fraîche

a few dashes of chilli sauce (mild Chinese style or Tabasco sauce)

salt and freshly ground black pepper

1 Cook the linguine or tagliatelle in lightly salted boiling water according to the pack instructions. Drain, rinse in cold water for a few moments and then return it to the pan.

2 Heat the sweetcorn either in the microwave or in a small saucepan. Mix it into the pasta along with the spring onions.

3 Beat the crab and crème fraîche together to make a smooth mixture, and add chilli sauce to taste. Stir the crab mixture into the pasta. Reheat the pasta gently, season to taste and serve immediately.

HERB AND LIME SALMON

8 Points per recipe

Serves: 2
Preparation time: 5 minutes
Cooking time: 15 minutes
Calories per serving: 190
Freezing: not recommended

Salmon is a very healthy fish as it is high in omega 3 fatty acids, which are excellent for your heart and blood cholesterol. This is a simple idea for a quick and tasty meal. Serve with 200 g (7 oz) baby new potatoes or 100 g (3½ oz) plain boiled rice, each adding 2 Points per serving.

---

2 × 100 g (3½ oz) fresh salmon fillets
1 spring onion, chopped
2 large sprigs of fresh dill
juice of 1 lime
1 teaspoon low fat spread
salt and freshly ground black pepper

---

1 Preheat the grill. Check the fish for any pin bones, and pull these out with tweezers or with your fingernails.
2 Grill the salmon steaks for about 5 minutes on each side, or until the flesh feels firm when pressed with the back of a fork. Season the steaks well, place them on two plates and keep them warm.

3 Put the spring onion, dill, lime juice and low fat spread in a small saucepan. Add a splash of water to moisten the sauce a little. Heat the mixture until it just starts to bubble and then spoon it over the fish. Serve immediately.

Top tip There's a knack to cooking fish just right. If it's overcooked it will become dry. It's cooked when it feels just firm – not solid. There should be a very slight bounce to it.

SWEETCORN RISOTTO

7½ Points per recipe

(v) if using vegetable stock

Serves: 1
Preparation time: 5 minutes
Cooking time: 25 minutes
Calories per serving: 575
Freezing: not recommended

Risotto made with Arborio rice makes a wonderful one pot meal – tasty and very satisfying. The preparation is simple and of course, there is only one saucepan to wash up!

---

low fat cooking spray
1 small red onion, chopped
1 large garlic clove, chopped
75 g (2¾ oz) Arborio rice
350 ml (12 fl oz) boiling vegetable or chicken stock

---

170 g can of sweetcorn, drained and liquid reserved
1 tablespoon chopped fresh parsley
1 tablespoon grated Parmesan cheese
salt and freshly ground black pepper

---

1 Heat a medium size saucepan and spray it with low fat cooking spray. Cook the onion and garlic with 2 tablespoons of water until they sizzle. Cover and cook for 5 minutes.
2 Remove the cover, stir in the rice and cook for 1 minute. Stir in a quarter of the hot stock and season. Bring the pan to the boil and cook, stirring, until the stock is absorbed.
3 Add another quarter of stock and stir until it is absorbed. Repeat this process twice more until all the stock is used up. This should take about 15 minutes.

4 Stir in the sweetcorn and the reserved liquid, and bring the pan to the boil. Add the parsley and half the Parmesan cheese. Check the seasoning, and serve the risotto hot, sprinkled with the remaining cheese.

Top tips To make the risotto ahead of time, par-cook it for 10 minutes, using half the stock, and then cool it. Finish by reheating the remaining stock and continuing the recipe.

Use proper risotto rice (Arborio or Carnaroli) for risottos. No other kind will give you that creaminess that makes risottos so delicious.

CHINESE STEAMED CHICKEN

2 Points per recipe

Serves: 1

Preparation time: 10 minutes

Cooking time: 15 minutes

Calories per serving: 160

Freezing: not recommended

This dish uses the Chinese method of steaming which is ideal for producing a fast and tasty meal – the steaming juices making a delicious, tangy sauce for the chicken. Serve this with zero Point, colourful vegetables that you have also steamed, and arrange them around the chicken. If you are feeling hungry you could have this with 150 g (5½ oz) plain boiled rice, adding an extra 3 Points.

100 g (3½ oz) skinless, boneless chicken breast

1 tablespoon light soy sauce

2 teaspoons dry sherry

1 pak choi (Chinese cabbage), halved or 50 g (1¾ oz) fresh Chinese leaf, shredded

a good pinch of Chinese five spice powder

½ teaspoon sesame oil

1 spring onion, sliced into long thin strips

salt and freshly ground black pepper

1 With a sharp knife, slash the chicken breast twice on each side. Toss it in a polythene food bag with the soy sauce and sherry, and then set aside to marinate for 5 minutes.

2 Meanwhile, place some water in the base of a saucepan and put it on the hob to boil. Place a metal or traditional bamboo steamer basket on top.

3 Lay the pak choi or Chinese leaf on a heatproof plate or a shallow bowl that is small enough to fit inside the basket and sprinkle over some seasoning. Put the chicken breast on top and trickle over the marinade juices. Sprinkle over the five spice powder. Spoon over the sesame oil and arrange the spring onion strips on top of the chicken.

4 Carefully place the plate or bowl inside the steamer. Cover and steam for 10 minutes or until the chicken breast feels firm when pressed. Carefully remove the plate or bowl from the steamer, making sure the steam does not burn your hand. Serve on a warmed plate.

This Pasta Arabiatta is just 5½ Points per serving and combines the sweet and smoky flavours of tomatoes and bacon.

PASTA ARABIATTA

5½ POINTS

11 Points per recipe

Serves: 2

Preparation time: 5 minutes

Cooking time: 15 minutes

Calories per serving: 405

Freezing: recommended

This is a fast and fabulous version of the classic Italian recipe. It's wonderfully low in Points and deliciously high in flavour.

2 rashers lean smoked back bacon, trimmed of excess fat and chopped into strips

1 teaspoon olive oil

1 large garlic clove, chopped

½–1 teaspoon dried chilli flakes

400 g can of chopped tomatoes with herbs

150 g (5½ oz) pasta shapes or spaghetti

salt and freshly ground black pepper

1 tablespoon chopped fresh parsley, to serve

1 Heat a non stick medium size saucepan until you can feel a good heat rising. Add the bacon and oil, and cook on a medium heat for 2 minutes.

2 Add the garlic and enough chilli flakes to suit your taste, and then cook for a further 2 minutes. Stir in the tomatoes and seasoning, and cook for 10 minutes, stirring once or twice.

3 Meanwhile, cook the pasta in lightly salted, boiling water for about 8 minutes or according to the pack instructions. Drain it and then mix in the tomato and chilli sauce. Serve the pasta sprinkled with the parsley.

Chinese Steamed Chicken – a delicious Oriental dish for just 2 Points!

Light Spaghetti Carbonara: a creamy, filling pasta dish for just 8 Points.

LIGHT SPAGHETTI CARBONARA

(8 POINTS)

8 Points per recipe
Serves: 1
Preparation time: 5 minutes
Cooking time: 15 minutes
Calories per serving: 490
Freezing: not recommended

This popular, creamy bacon pasta sauce can often be extremely high in Points. This recipe shows you how to make a lighter version that is just as tasty, but much healthier – perfect if you're following the Time to Eat Programme.

75 g (2¾ oz) spaghetti
1 egg yolk
5 tablespoons semi-skimmed milk
½ teaspoon cornflour
2 teaspoons grated Parmesan cheese
low fat cooking spray
1 rasher lean smoked back bacon, trimmed of fat and cut into fine strips
1 garlic clove, chopped
salt and freshly ground black pepper

1 Cook the spaghetti in lightly salted, boiling water according to the pack instructions. Drain the pasta, remove it from the pan and set it aside.
2 Meanwhile, beat the egg yolk, milk, cornflour and 1 teaspoon of the Parmesan cheese together in a cup.
3 Spray the same pasta pan with low fat cooking spray and stir fry the bacon strips and garlic for about 2 minutes. Return the pasta to the pan. Add seasoning and reheat the mixture, stirring, until it is piping hot.
4 Add the egg and milk mixture to the pan, stirring well until the mixture just starts to thicken. Remove the pan from the heat.
5 Pile the pasta into a shallow bowl and sprinkle with the remaining cheese before eating.

Top tip Don't over drain pasta. Keep it moist and you won't need to use as much sauce or oil.

Variation You can make a wonderful vegetarian version of this pasta classic simply by substituting 50 g (1¾ oz) sliced and blanched mushrooms for the bacon. The Points per serving will be 6½.

FISH AND LEEK PASTA

(6 POINTS)

6 Points per recipe
Serves: 1
Preparation time: 10 minutes
Cooking time: 15 minutes
Calories per serving: 495
Freezing: recommended

A filling and tasty fish supper, that is terrific after a busy day as a quick and easy meal for one.

1 leek, sliced thinly
1 small carrot, grated coarsely
250 ml (9 fl oz) skimmed milk
1 teaspoon cornflour
75 g (2¾ oz) skinless cod fillet, cut into small chunks
a pinch of dried mixed herbs
75 g (2¾ oz) pasta shapes
1–2 teaspoons fresh lemon juice
salt and freshly ground black pepper
1–2 teaspoons fresh chopped parsley, to serve (optional)

1 Place the leek and carrot in enough lightly salted, boiling water just to cover them. Blanch them for 3 minutes and then drain.
2 Blend the milk with the cornflour and bring this mixture to the boil in a non stick saucepan. Place the fish chunks in the pan, and add the dried herbs and seasoning. Reduce the heat and simmer for 5 minutes.
3 Stir the leek and carrot into the pan and heat them through for 1 minute or so. Check the seasoning and set aside.
4 Meanwhile, boil the pasta according to the packet instructions. Drain it and then stir it into the fish mixture. Add the lemon juice to taste. Serve piping hot in a shallow bowl and sprinkle over some chopped parsley, if desired.

Variations Try other white fish like hoki, hake, haddock and whiting as an alternative to cod. The Points per serving will be 6, 6, 5½ and 6 respectively.

White sauce made this way with cornflour is simple to do and when made with skimmed milk is really low in Points. You can even adapt it to make a sweet sauce – just add artificial sweetener to taste and a few drops of vanilla or rum essence.

LAMB STEAK PROVENCAL

3½ Points per recipe

Serves: 1
Preparation time: 10 minutes
Cooking time: 20 minutes
Calories per serving: 315
Freezing: not recommended

The wonderful fresh tomato and courgette sauce in this recipe, complements lamb perfectly, drawing out its delicate flavours. This is delicious served with a small portion of chips for an extra 4½ Points.

2 fresh tomatoes
1 large garlic clove, crushed
2 spring onions, chopped
1 courgette, chopped
3 tablespoons dry white wine
1 sprig of fresh basil, chopped or ½ teaspoon dried basil
125 g (4½ oz) lean lamb steak
salt and freshly ground black pepper

1 With a sharp knife, score small crosses in the base of the tomatoes, and then place them in a bowl of just boiled water. Remove them after 30 seconds, and then slip off the skins. Quarter the tomatoes, remove the cores, and chop the flesh.
2 Place the tomatoes in a medium size saucepan with the garlic, spring onions, courgette, wine and seasoning. If you are using dried basil add it at this stage. Cook the mixture until it sizzles. Reduce the heat, cover and simmer gently for 10 minutes until the vegetables have softened. If you are using fresh basil, mix it in at this stage.
3 Meanwhile, preheat the grill. Season the lamb steak and grill it for about 5 minutes on each side. Alternatively, you can cook it on a non stick griddle pan. If you like the lamb slightly pink cook it until it feels lightly springy, or, if you like it well done, cook it until the meat is firm.
4 Spoon the sauce over the lamb to serve.

Variations Try this recipe using beef, pork or turkey steaks – it will work equally well. The Points per serving will be 3, 3 and 2½ respectively.

If you don't want to use wine you can substitute water. You will save ½ Point per serving.

Use this sauce for pasta. Make a double quantity and freeze in two single portions.

CHICKEN PILAFF

11½ Points per recipe

Serves: 2
Preparation time: 10 minutes
Cooking time: 20 minutes
Calories per serving: 455
Freezing: recommended

This is a great one pot meal as the meat, vegetables and rice are all cooked together. Use easy cook basmati for its special flavour. If you are cooking this just for yourself, save half and freeze it for another day.

3 spring onions, chopped
½ small green pepper, de-seeded and chopped
1 small carrot, grated coarsely
low fat cooking spray
2 teaspoons garlic purée
150 g (5½ oz) chicken breast, cubed
1 teaspoon mild or medium curry powder
150 g (5½ oz) easy cook basmati rice
400 ml (14 fl oz) chicken stock
100 g (3½ oz) frozen peas
salt and freshly ground black pepper
2 tablespoons very low fat plain yogurt, to serve

1 Heat a large saucepan. Spray the spring onions, pepper and carrot with low fat cooking spray and add to the pan along with the garlic purée and 4 tablespoons of water. Cook this mixture until it sizzles, and then cover and simmer for 3 minutes.
2 Remove the cover and stir the chicken into the pan along with the curry powder. Heat for 1 minute or so until the meat is sealed, stirring once or twice.
3 Add the rice, and then stir in the stock and seasoning. Bring to the boil, stirring. Reduce the heat, cover the pan and cook for 15 minutes until the liquid is absorbed and the chicken is cooked.
4 Mix in the peas, check the seasoning and reheat for 2 minutes until the peas are piping hot. Serve the pilaff on two warmed plates, each topped with a tablespoon of yogurt.

Variation For a vegetarian option substitute cubes of tofu for the chicken breast and use vegetable stock. You will save ½ Point per serving.

Lamb Steak Provençal and chips: all this for just 8 Points.

Spicy Fish Burger in a bun – all for just 4 Points.

family meals

Increasingly, as people become more health conscious they want to feed their whole family well balanced, nutritious meals. This chapter shows you how to do this, while staying within your Points allowance. These recipes are full of flavour and taste – so are perfect for all the family.

SPICY FISH BURGERS

(2 POINTS)

7¹/₂ Points per recipe

Serves: 4

Preparation and cooking time: 25 minutes

Calories per serving: 135

Freezing: recommended

Smoked fish tastes delicious in these burgers. They take hardly any time to prepare and cook. Serve each burger with a crisp zero Point green salad and a medium size bun, adding the 2 extra Points.

300 g (10¹/₂ oz) skinless cod fillet

200 g (7 oz) skinless smoked cod fillet

1 small onion, chopped

1 teaspoon mild curry powder

low fat cooking spray

salt and freshly ground black pepper

1 lime, quartered, to serve

For the cucumber relish

¹/₄ cucumber

150 g tub of low fat plain yogurt

1 tablespoon chopped fresh dill or

¹/₂ teaspoon dried dill

salt and freshly ground black pepper

1 With your fingertips, check the fish for any bones and pull out any you can feel. Cut the flesh into chunks. Place the fish in a food processor with the onion, curry powder and half a teaspoon each of salt and pepper. Process the mixture in short bursts, scraping down the sides once or twice, until it becomes a chunky paste – don't over process it.

2 Divide the mixture into four smooth balls, and then flatten them into burger shapes. Chill them in the refrigerator until required.

3 Meanwhile, make the relish. Halve the cucumber and scoop out the seeds with a teaspoon. Chop the flesh finely or coarsely grate it. Mix it with the yogurt, dill and seasoning. Chill the relish in the refrigerator until you need it.

4 When you are ready to cook the burgers, heat a large non stick frying pan and spray it with low fat cooking spray. Add the burgers to the pan and cook them for about 3–4 minutes on each side, turning them carefully, until golden brown and firm when pressed.

5 Serve the fish burgers with a lime quarter for each serving and the cucumber relish.

Top tip Open freeze these burgers and then store in plastic bags in the freezer. That way they won't stick together and can be eaten one at a time.

Variation Any smoked or white fish works well in these burgers, e.g. haddock, whiting or hake, but remember to alter the Points accordingly.

TANGY LAMB CHOPS WITH IRISH MASH

18½ Points per recipe

Serves: 4

Preparation time: 10 minutes

Cooking time: 20 minutes

Calories per serving: 405

Freezing: recommended for mash only

Creamy mashed potato is a great Irish family dish, and the juicy, tangy glazed lamb in this recipe accompanies it perfectly. Serve with zero Point grilled tomatoes.

750 g (1 lb 10 oz) potatoes, peeled and cut into chunks

150 ml (¼ pint) skimmed milk

1 teaspoon low fat spread

4 × 100 g (3½ oz) lamb chump chops, trimmed of excess fat

½ medium green cabbage, cored and shredded

4 spring onions, chopped

freshly ground nutmeg

4 teaspoons BBQ or brown sauce

salt and freshly ground black pepper

1 Cook the potatoes in lightly salted, boiling water for about 12 minutes, until tender. Drain well and return them to the pan. Mash the potatoes until smooth.

2 Heat the milk and low fat spread in a small saucepan. Add this to the potatoes and mix until you have a creamy consistency.

3 Meanwhile, preheat the grill. Season the lamb chops and grill for about 4 minutes on each side until the meat is almost firm.

4 While the lamb is grilling, cook the cabbage in lightly salted, boiling water for 5 minutes and then drain it.

5 Mix the cabbage and spring onions into the mash, and then season with the nutmeg, salt and pepper to taste.

Reheat the mash gently if necessary.

6 Spread a teaspoon of BBQ or brown sauce on one side of each chump chop. Return them to the grill for 1 more minute until the glaze bubbles.

7 Divide the mashed potato mixture between four warmed plates and arrange a chop on top of each.

Top tip For perfect mashed potatoes choose a good variety such as Maris Piper, Desiree or King Edwards.

Variation Jazz up mashed potatoes with some interesting flavours. Try coarse grain mustard, horseradish or Worcestershire sauce, remembering to alter the Points accordingly. You can also make the mash substituting carrots or celeriac for half the potatoes. The Points per serving will then be 3½.

CHICKEN KEBABS WITH FRESH CARROT RELISH

8 Points per recipe

Serves: 4

Preparation time: 10 minutes

Cooking time: 15 minutes

Calories per serving: 160

Freezing: not recommended

These tangy and refreshing kebabs are great cooked on the barbecue in summer.

1 red onion, quartered

4 × 125 g (4½ oz) skinless chicken breasts, cut into 2 cm (¾ inch) cubes

½ teaspoon dried mixed herbs

1 green pepper, de-seeded and cut into 2 cm (¾ inch) squares

salt and freshly ground black pepper

For the carrot relish

2 medium carrots, grated coarsely

juice of 1 small lemon

1 tablespoon chopped fresh mint or parsley

salt and freshly ground black pepper

1 First make the relish. Mix the carrots with the lemon juice, mint or parsley and seasoning. Let it stand for 10–15 minutes to allow the carrots to soften.

2 Meanwhile, divide the onion into its individual layers. Sprinkle the chicken with the dried herbs and mix well to coat the pieces. Thread the meat, onion and pepper, in turn, on to four metal or bamboo skewers, and season them lightly. Preheat the grill.

3 Grill the kebabs for about 12 minutes, turning them once. Keep

a mug of water at the ready and brush the meat as it cooks – do this about 3 or 4 times during cooking as it helps to moisten the meat. When cooked, the meat should feel firm when pressed.

4 Divide the relish between four plates. Serve the kebabs on top.

Top tip Fresh vegetable relishes make excellent no Point accompaniments. Try finely chopped fresh cucumber and tomato; add some seasoning, a pinch or two of ground cumin and some freshly chopped parsley or mint. Allow to stand for 10 minutes before serving.

Variation For a vegetarian alternative substitute Quorn pieces for the chicken. The Points will then be 1½ per serving.

TUNA PASTA BAKE

26½ Points per recipe

Serves: 4

Preparation time: 5 minutes

Cooking time: 20 minutes

Calories per serving: 420

Freezing: recommended

A great family favourite from America, this quick, budget dish is bound to please everyone, and the all in one sauce is so easy to make – fantastic!

---

250 g (9 oz) pasta shapes

1 onion, chopped

400 ml (14 fl oz) skimmed milk

2 tablespoons cornflour

100 g (3½ oz) frozen peas, defrosted

200 g can of tuna in brine, drained and flaked

50 g (1¾ oz) half fat Cheddar cheese, grated

15 g (½ oz) Parmesan cheese, grated

2 tablespoons natural colour dried breadcrumbs

6–8 cherry tomatoes, halved

salt and freshly ground black pepper

1 Cook the pasta with the onion in a large saucepan of lightly salted, boiling water according to the pack instructions. Drain and rinse in cold water. Set it aside.

2 While the pasta is cooking, make the sauce. In a heatproof jug, mix 3 tablespoons of the milk with the cornflour to make a smooth paste. In a large saucepan, put the rest of the milk on to boil and when the liquid starts to creep up the sides of the pan, pour it over the cornflour paste, whisking as you do so.

3 Return the milk mixture to the pan and cook, stirring, on a low heat until it thickens. Add the peas and tuna, and then simmer for 2 minutes.

Remove the pan from the heat and cool slightly.

4 Mix in all the Cheddar cheese and half of the Parmesan cheese. Stir the cooked pasta into the sauce. Check the seasoning. Reheat it all gently in the pan but do not allow it to boil.

5 Preheat the grill. Transfer the pasta mixture to an ovenproof dish. Mix the remaining Parmesan cheese with the breadcrumbs and scatter this over the top. Arrange the tomato halves, cut side up, over the breadcrumb topping.

6 Place the dish under the grill and cook until the top is crispy and golden. Serve on four warmed plates.

Tuna Pasta Bake: it's tasty, satisfying and couldn't be easier to put together! 6½ Points per serving.

Italian Roast Chicken served with a medium jacket potato. Absolutely delicious – and all for 9 Points.

ITALIAN ROAST CHICKEN

26 Points per recipe

Serves: 4
Preparation time: 5 minutes
Cooking time: 25 minutes
Calories per serving: 180
Freezing: not recommended

This recipe shows you how to give a tasty twist to the traditional roast. The whole family will love it! Serve this chicken with a crisp green zero Point salad and a medium jacket potato for an extra 2½ Points per serving.

8 × 75 g (2¾ oz) skinless, boneless chicken thighs, trimmed of fat
2 teaspoons low fat spread
2 teaspoons mild chilli powder
½ teaspoon dried oregano or basil
salt and freshly ground black pepper
1 lemon, quartered, to serve

1 Arrange the chicken thighs in a shallow baking dish. Preheat the oven to Gas Mark 4/180°C/fan oven 160°C.

2 Beat together the low fat spread, chilli powder, herbs and ½ teaspoon of salt. Dab this mixture on top of the thighs.

3 Season the chicken with pepper and then cover the baking dish loosely with foil. Bake for 20–25 minutes, until the chicken is tender and cooked through.

4 Divide the chicken between four serving plates. Pour over any remaining cooking juices and serve each portion with a lemon quarter.

CHICKEN POT PIE

27½ Points per recipe

Serves: 4
Preparation time: 10 minutes
Cooking time: 20 minutes
Calories per serving: 235
Freezing: recommended

This recipe makes for a wonderful and warming family meal, and will satisfy you even on the hungriest of days.

2 teaspoons low fat spread
500 g (1 lb 2 oz) skinless, boneless chicken thighs, trimmed of fat and halved lengthways
1 carrot, sliced thinly
1 parsnip, chopped
1 celery stick, sliced thinly
1 leek, sliced thinly
1 large potato, scrubbed and chopped
½ teaspoon dried thyme
1 large bay leaf
1 teaspoon coarse grain mustard
2 teaspoons plain white flour
300 ml (½ pint) chicken or vegetable stock
salt and freshly ground black pepper

1 Melt the low fat spread in a cast iron casserole dish and sauté the chicken thigh pieces for about 3 minutes until browned.

2 Stir in the vegetables and 4 tablespoons of water. Cover and simmer for 5 minutes until the vegetables have softened. Mix in the thyme and bay leaf, and then add the mustard and flour, stirring well to blend them in. Stir in the stock. Season and bring the pan to the boil.

3 Reduce the heat, cover and simmer for 15 minutes until the meat and vegetables are tender. Serve on four warmed plates.

Top tip Mild and coarse grain mustard are great in sauces; they add a subtle bite without adding extra Points. Dijon mustards have a lovely, tangy flavour.

Chicken Pot Pie: a wonderful winter warmer – and only 7 Points.

HAM AND LEEK ROLLS IN PARSLEY SAUCE

4½ Points per recipe

Serves: 4
Preparation time: 10 minutes
Cooking time: 20 minutes
Calories per serving: 120
Freezing: not recommended

This is a lovely warming and satisfying farmhouse style supper dish. A golden, bubbling topping reveals a creamy leek and ham mixture underneath – absolutely delicious! Serve with 100 g (3½ oz) new potatoes – this will be 1 extra Point per serving.

4 thick leeks
2 teaspoons cornflour
300 ml (½ pint) skimmed milk
2 tablespoons chopped freshly parsley
1 teaspoon low fat spread
4 lean slices ham
2 tablespoons grated half fat Cheddar cheese
1 tomato, quartered, de-seeded and chopped
salt and freshly ground black pepper

1 Trim the roots and dark green stems of the leeks so you end up with lengths of about 17 cm (6½ inches). Blanch them in lightly salted, boiling water for 5 minutes. Drain them well and pat dry with kitchen paper.
2 Blend the cornflour with 2 tablespoons of the milk to form a paste. Put the rest of the milk in a saucepan and bring it to the boil. When the milk starts to bubble take the pan off the heat and stir in the cornflour paste. Return the pan to the heat and simmer, stirring, for about 1 minute until the sauce thickens.
3 Stir the parsley, low fat spread and seasoning into the sauce.
4 Preheat the oven to Gas Mark 6/ 200°C/fan oven 180°C. Wrap each leek in a slice of ham. Place the leek and ham rolls in a shallow dish with the join of the ham facing downwards. Pour over the sauce.
5 Mix the cheese with the chopped tomato and scatter this over the top. Bake for 15 minutes until the topping is golden and bubbling. Serve on four warmed plates.

Variation Try canned celery hearts, drained, instead of fresh leeks. The Points will remain the same.

PORK MEAT LOAF

5½ POINTS

21 Points per recipe

Serves: 4
Preparation time: 5 minutes
Cooking time: 25 minutes
Calories per serving: 295
Freezing: recommended

Minced pork is marvellously lean nowadays and is excellent used in this hot family style spicy meat loaf. Serve with pasta, rice or plain boiled potatoes, adding the extra Points.

1 medium slice white or wholemeal bread, crusts removed
500 g (1 lb 2 oz) minced pork
2 teaspoons garlic purée
1 teaspoon fine sea salt
½ teaspoon dried mixed herbs
2 tablespoons brown spicy sauce (e.g. HP sauce)
low fat cooking spray
2 long rashers of streaky bacon
freshly ground black pepper

1 Plunge the bread slice into a bowl of cold water, and then remove it and squeeze it dry. Place the wet bread in a large bowl and break it up with a fork.
2 Add the minced pork, garlic purée, the teaspoon of salt, black pepper to taste, dried mixed herbs and brown sauce to the bread. Mix it all together thoroughly.
3 Place a large sheet of foil on the base of a shallow roasting pan and spray it evenly with the low fat cooking spray. Cut the bacon rashers in half and place them in the centre of the foil.
4 Preheat the oven to Gas Mark 6/ 200°C/fan oven 180°C. Mound the minced pork mixture on top of the bacon, pressing and shaping it into a thick roll and wrapping the bacon around the mixture. Draw the foil sides up and scrunch them loosely together.
5 Bake the loaf in the oven for about 20 minutes, until the meat feels firm when pressed. Allow it to stand for 5 minutes. Serve the meat loaf in thick slices with any remaining cooking juices strained and poured over.

Top tip Freeze separate slices wrapped in cling film to eat another time.

Variation Try minced turkey or chicken instead of pork, but remember to alter the Points accordingly.

Ham and Leek Rolls in Parsley Sauce – a classic combination. Try it with new potatoes for just 2 Points.

Smoked Fish
Kedgeree with
Oven Roasted
Tomatoes – a
colourful dish with
a delicious flavour
for 5 Points.

TAGLIATELLE WITH LENTIL AND MUSHROOM SAUCE

19½ Points per recipe

Ⓥ Serves: 4

Preparation time: 10 minutes

Cooking time: 20 minutes

Calories per serving: 340

Freezing: recommended for the sauce

Lentils are great for a quick and nourishing meat free meal, and taste particularly good in this pasta sauce. Serve it with freshly cooked zero Point cabbage or green beans.

1 large onion, chopped

2 teaspoons garlic purée

1 carrot, grated coarsely

250 g (9 oz) mushrooms, chopped finely

2 teaspoons olive oil

½ teaspoon dried oregano or marjoram

230 g can of chopped tomatoes

400 g can of red lentils, drained and rinsed

200 g (7 oz) tagliatelle

salt and freshly ground black pepper

To serve

4 tablespoons quark

2 teaspoons freshly grated Parmesan cheese

1 Mix the onion, garlic purée, carrot, mushrooms and olive oil in a large saucepan, and then add 4 tablespoons water. Heat this mixture until it sizzles. Cover the pan and simmer for 10 minutes until the vegetables have softened, stirring once or twice.

2 Season and add the herbs, the tomatoes and lentils. Cook, uncovered, until all the liquid has evaporated and the mixture has thickened – this will take about 10 minutes. Check the seasoning.

3 Meanwhile, cook the tagliatelle in lightly salted, boiling water according to the pack instructions. Drain and mix it with the sauce. Serve in four warmed bowls and top each serving of pasta with 1 tablespoon of quark or fromage frais and ½ teaspoon of Parmesan cheese.

Variations You can replace the lentils with the same quantity of canned chick peas. The Points per serving will remain the same.

You can also turn the lentil sauce into a quick cannelloni. Cook 200 g (7 oz) lasagne sheets in boiling water for 5 minutes. Drain and pat dry. Spread the sauce over the pasta and roll up each sheet. Top with 4 tablespoons quark or very low fat fromage frais and 2 teaspoons freshly grated Parmesan. The Points per serving will remain the same.

SMOKED FISH KEDGEREE WITH OVEN ROASTED TOMATOES

19½ Points per recipe

Serves: 4

Preparation time: 10 minutes

Cooking time: 20 minutes

Calories per serving: 365

Freezing: not recommended

Fish and rice makes a healthy and filling combination. In this low Point version of the traditional dish, you put tomatoes in the oven to roast while you make the kedgeree. The juicy roasted tomatoes add moisture to the dish, so you don't need to add lots of cream and butter and you don't pile on the Points!

4 medium tomatoes

4 pinches caster sugar

4 pinches dried thyme or mixed herbs

500 ml (18 fl oz) boiling water

300 g (10½ oz) smoked haddock fillets

250 g (9 oz) basmati rice

½ teaspoon salt

3 spring onions, chopped

1 teaspoon mild curry powder

2 teaspoons low fat spread

salt and freshly ground black pepper

2 eggs, hard boiled and quartered

1 Preheat the oven to Gas Mark 4/ 180°C/fan oven 160°C. Halve the tomatoes widthways and place them, cut side up, in a shallow dish. Sprinkle the halves with the sugar, herbs and seasoning.

2 Bake the tomatoes for 12–15 minutes, until they are just softened. Remove them from the oven and let them cool.

3 Meanwhile, make the kedgeree. Add the boiling water to a frying pan or other shallow pan. Add the fish and cook over a gentle heat until the flesh is just firm, this will take about 5 minutes.

4 Pour off the cooking water into a large saucepan. Skin and flake the fish, checking for any bones.

5 Stir the rice into the hot water and add ½ teaspoon of salt. Bring the pan to the boil, while stirring. Reduce the heat, cover and simmer for 10 minutes.

6 When the rice is cooked, mix in the spring onions, curry powder and low fat spread. Stir in the fish and check the seasoning.

7 Divide the kedgeree between four warmed plates and top each serving with two egg quarters. Serve each portion with 2 halves of the roasted tomatoes.

QUICK TURKEY COTTAGE PIE

18½ Points per recipe

Serves: 4

Preparation time: 10 minutes

Cooking time: 20 minutes

Calories per serving: 265

Freezing: recommended

This wholesome and satisfying supper dish is great served with zero Point green beans and carrots. It's wonderful for all the family and is great for a cosy evening meal.

500 g (1 lb 2 oz) potatoes, peeled and cubed

4 tablespoons hot skimmed milk

1 tablespoon chopped fresh parsley or ¼ teaspoon ground nutmeg (optional)

500 g pack of turkey mince

low fat cooking spray

2 garlic cloves, crushed

½ teaspoon dried thyme, oregano or mixed herbs

4 spring onions, chopped

1 tablespoon white flour

500 ml (18 fl oz) chicken stock

1 tablespoon dried natural colour breadcrumbs

salt and freshly ground black pepper

1 Cook the potatoes in lightly salted, boiling water for 10–12 minutes, until just tender. Drain well and then mash them until smooth.

2 Beat in the hot milk, parsley or nutmeg, if using, and seasoning. Set the mash aside.

3 Meanwhile, heat a large non stick frying pan and add the mince in small amounts, stirring quickly to break it up. Spray the mince with low fat cooking spray and cook until it becomes crumbly.

4 Add the crushed garlic, herbs and spring onions. Cook for 2 minutes, and then sprinkle in the flour and mix it in.

5 Now, stir in the stock and raise the heat. Simmer for 10 minutes until the mixture has thickened and reduced down. Season well.

6 Preheat the grill. Spoon the mince mixture into an ovenproof dish. Spoon over the potatoes, spreading them evenly with a fork. Sprinkle over the breadcrumbs.

7 Place the dish under the grill until the top turns lightly golden. Serve on four warmed plates.

Variation For an even quicker meal, serve the mince on its own with the potatoes, plain boiled and sprinkled with chopped parsley.

BEEF AND PEA KEEMA

22 Points per recipe

Serves: 4

Preparation time: 5 minutes

Cooking time: 20 minutes

Calories per serving: 300

Freezing: recommended

This is a quick and tasty Indian style dish of beef and peas. Serve this with 4 tablespoons of cooked rice for an extra 3 Points.

low fat cooking spray

500 g pack of extra lean beef mince

2 large garlic cloves, chopped

1 bunch of spring onions, chopped

2–3 teaspoons mild or medium curry powder

1 tablespoon mango chutney

1 tablespoon white flour

300 ml (½ pint) beef stock

125 g (4½ oz) frozen peas

salt and freshly ground black pepper

To serve

150 g low fat plain yogurt

1–2 tablespoons chopped fresh coriander or parsley

1 Heat a non stick wok or frying pan. When you can feel a good heat rising spray the pan with the cooking spray. Add the mince in small amounts, stirring quickly to break it up. Cook until the meat is browned and crumbly.

2 Add the garlic and spring onions, and cook for 2 minutes. Stir in the curry powder and cook for 1 minute.

3 Mix in the mango chutney and flour, and then slowly stir in the stock. Season and bring to the boil while stirring. Reduce the heat and simmer for 10 minutes.

4 Add the peas to the pan and cook for 3 more minutes. Serve hot topped with the yogurt and chopped coriander or parsley.

Top tip When freezing this dish omit the yogurt and fresh herbs.

Variations Try making this dish with turkey mince, the Points would then be 4 per serving.

For a vegetarian alternative replace the beef mince with Quorn mince. The Points per serving will be 3.

Quick Turkey Cottage Pie – a family favourite for just 4½ Points.

Spinach and Cheese Rolls: a wonderful combination wrapped in pastry for an unbelievable 1½ Points.

vegetarian

Whether you are a vegetarian by conviction or simply enjoy eating the wonderful variety of colourful and healthy dishes that just happen to be meat and fish free, you should find some inspirational dishes in this section. Take time to try out some new foods like tofu (soya bean curd) and Quorn – both man made, high protein foods which are very low in Points and are wonderfully adaptable.

SPINACH AND CHEESE ROLLS

6¹/₂ Points per recipe

Ⓥ Serves: 4

Preparation time: 10 minutes

Cooking time: 15 minutes

Calories per serving: 135

Freezing: not recommended

Creamy spinach rolled into light and crispy filo pastry makes a tasty and attractive meal. Serve these rolls warm with a zero Point green salad and sliced tomato.

250 g pack of baby spinach leaves

200 g tub of reduced fat cottage cheese, ideally with chives

1 tablespoon chopped fresh dill or 1 teaspoon dried dill

4 × 30 cm × 17 cm (12 inch × 6¹/₂ inch) sheets of filo pastry

1 tablespoon low fat spread, melted

salt and freshly ground black pepper

1 Cook the spinach according to the pack instructions, either in the microwave or in a large saucepan. Drain it well, pressing out as much water as possible.

2 Chop the spinach finely, and then mix it with the cottage cheese, dill and seasoning.

3 Preheat the oven to Gas Mark 6/ 200°C/fan oven 180°C. Using a pastry brush, dab the filo sheets with the melted low fat spread. Divide the spinach filling into four and place along the bottom of each sheet, spreading it out to flatten it slightly. Roll each sheet up firmly, but not too tightly.

4 Place the rolls on a non stick baking sheet. Bake them for 15 minutes until they are crisp and golden. Slice them in half on the diagonal and serve them warm.

Variation This spinach and cottage cheese filling works brilliantly in jacket potatoes, but remember to alter the Points accordingly.

MOROCCAN STEW WITH GREEN HERB COUSCOUS

20 Points per recipe

Ⓥ Ⓥⓖ Serves: 4

Preparation time: 15 minutes

Cooking time: 20 minutes

Calories per serving: 350

Freezing: recommended, but freeze stew and couscous separately

Vegetable and bean stews are quick to make, and tasty for vegetarians and meat eaters alike. Couscous makes a great store cupboard standby and is very easy to prepare.

1 large onion, chopped
1 carrot, sliced thinly
2 teaspoons garlic purée
1 tablespoon ginger purée or freshly grated ginger (optional)
1 large fresh green chilli, de-seeded and chopped
2 teaspoons olive oil
1 teaspoon ground cumin
2 teaspoons ground coriander
1 teaspoon ground paprika

¼ teaspoon ground cinnamon
a good pinch of dried saffron strands or ¼ teaspoon turmeric (optional)
400 g can of chopped tomatoes
1 medium courgette, chopped
400 g can of chick peas, drained and liquid reserved
salt and freshly ground black pepper

For the couscous

200 g (7 oz) couscous
400 ml (14 fl oz) boiling water
1 teaspoon extra virgin olive oil
1 teaspoon salt
2 tablespoons chopped fresh parsley
1 tablespoon chopped fresh dill or coriander
freshly ground black pepper

1 First, start preparing the couscous. Put the couscous grains in a big bowl and pour over the boiling water. Add the olive oil, the salt and freshly ground pepper to taste. Stir well and allow to cool, stirring occasionally with a fork to separate the grains.

2 For the stew, put the onion, carrot, garlic purée, ginger (if using) and chilli into a large saucepan with the oil and 4 tablespoons of water. Heat this mixture until it starts to sizzle, and then cover the pan and simmer for 10 minutes.

3 Remove the cover and stir in the cumin, coriander, paprika, cinnamon and saffron or turmeric, if using. Cook for 1 minute. Add the canned tomatoes, courgette, chick peas with the reserved liquid and seasoning. Bring the pan to the boil and simmer for about 5 minutes until the courgette is tender.

4 Meanwhile, cover the couscous and reheat it in the microwave on High for 5 minutes. Alternatively, preheat the oven to Gas Mark 4/180°C/fan oven 160°C, place the couscous in an ovenproof dish, covered with foil, and heat for 10 minutes. When the couscous is piping hot, stir in the chopped herbs.

5 Serve the couscous with the stew spooned on top.

CHINESE OMELETTE

3½ Points per recipe

Ⓥ Serves: 1

Preparation and cooking time: 15 minutes

Calories per serving: 270

Freezing: not recommended

A great main meal dish that gives a simple recipe a wonderful Oriental flavour. Serve this with a zero Point salad of watercress or rocket.

1 medium tomato
1 spring onion, chopped
50 g (1¾ oz) cooked rice

2 eggs
1 tablespoon light soy sauce
low fat cooking spray
freshly ground black pepper

1 Halve the tomato and scoop out the seeds. Remove the core and chop the flesh. Mix it together with the spring onion and rice.

2 Beat the eggs with the soy sauce and black pepper.

3 Spray a small non stick omelette pan with the low fat cooking spray. Place it on the hob and when you can feel a good heat rising immediately pour in the eggs and cook them on a medium heat. Stir them occasionally, until the mixture starts to set.

4 Mix in the vegetable and rice mixture and continue to stir occasionally, until the eggs are lightly set. Fold the omelette in half and slide it out of the pan on to a warmed plate.

Top tip Freeze any leftover cooked rice, and use it to add spoonfuls to soups and omelettes to make them more filling and substantial.

Variation Thinly slice a leek and blanch in boiling water for 2 minutes. Drain well and use instead of the tomato and onion. You can also mix in 2 finely chopped mushrooms as well – there's no need to cook them.

BROCCOLI AND BLUE CHEESE PASTA

7½ POINTS

14½ Points per recipe

Ⓥ Serves: 2

Preparation time: 5 minutes

Cooking time: 15 minutes

Calories per serving: 455

Freezing: not recommended

Blue cheese has a full flavour so a little goes a long way. It's great for adding a superb taste to pasta without adding too many extra Points.

---

100 g (3½ oz) pasta shapes

250 g (9 oz) broccoli

170 g can of sweetcorn, drained

300 ml (½ pint) skimmed milk

1 tablespoon cornflour

50 g (1¾ oz) firm blue cheese (e.g. Stilton)

a good pinch of dried mixed herbs

salt and freshly ground black pepper

---

1 Cook the pasta in lightly salted, boiling water according to the pack instructions. Drain and rinse it in cold water, and then tip it into a big bowl.

2 Chop the stalk of the broccoli and cut the florets into small pieces. In lightly salted, boiling water blanch the pieces of stalk for 3 minutes, and then add the florets and cook for another 2 minutes. Drain, and mix the broccoli and sweetcorn with the pasta.

3 In a heatproof jug, blend a little milk with the cornflour to make a paste. Pour the rest of the milk in a saucepan and bring it to the boil. When it starts to bubble, pour it over the blended cornflour, whisking continuously. Return the mixture to the pan and stir it over a low heat until it thickens.

4 Remove the pan from the heat and crumble the cheese into the sauce. Add the herbs and seasoning.

5 Mix together the pasta mixture with the sauce, and heat gently until bubbling. Serve immediately.

Top tip If you love blue cheese, then look out for the traditional British cheese, Blue Vinney, which is naturally lower in Points than others. It is now sold in most supermarkets.

Variation Substitute 100 g (3½ oz) halved baby new potatoes for the pasta. The Points will be reduced to 5½ per serving.

Broccoli and Blue Cheese Pasta is a wonderfully creamy and cheesy dish for 7½ Points.

Stir fry with noodles: it's full of delicious Oriental flavours and is just 3 Points.

STIR FRY WITH NOODLES

6 Points per recipe

Ⓥ Serves: 2

Preparation and cooking time:
20 minutes

Calories per serving: 275

Freezing: not recommended

This tasty stir fry makes a great light lunch.

100 g (3¹/₂ oz) egg noodles
100 g (3¹/₂ oz) mange tout peas
100 g (3¹/₂ oz) baby sweetcorn, halved
125 g (4¹/₂ oz) button mushrooms, halved
low fat cooking spray
1 large garlic clove, crushed
1 teaspoon cornflour
1–2 tablespoons light soy sauce
1 tablespoon dry sherry (optional)
¹/₂ teaspoon sesame oil
salt and freshly ground black pepper
a good pinch of sesame seeds, to serve

1 Soak or cook the noodles according to the pack instructions.
2 Meanwhile, mix together the mange tout peas, baby sweetcorn and mushrooms. Heat a wok or a large frying pan and spray the base with low fat cooking spray. When you can feel a good heat rising add the vegetables. Add 2–3 tablespoons of water if the mixture becomes dry.
3 Stir fry for about 3–5 minutes, until the vegetables soften. Add the garlic and cook for 1 minute more. Mix the cornflour with the soy sauce, sherry, if using, sesame oil and 100 ml (3½ fl oz) water.
4 Mix the blended cornflour into the pan and stir until you have a smooth and glossy mixture. Check the seasoning. Add the noodles and serve sprinkled lightly with sesame seeds.

BALTI VEGETABLES AND WHOLE SPICE PILAFF

11¹/₂ Points per recipe

Ⓥ Ⓥ₉ Serves: 2

Preparation time: 5 minutes

Cooking time: 25 minutes

Calories per serving: 460

Freezing: not recommended

Make your own Balti curry served with an easy cook basmati pilaff, cooked in the traditional way with whole spices that are easy to pick out after cooking – all the authentic flavour, with little of the traditional Points!

1 tablespoon desiccated coconut
300 ml (¹/₂ pint) boiling water
1 medium onion, chopped into wedges
1 carrot, chopped
1 celery stick, sliced thinly
2 teaspoons garlic purée
1 tablespoon ginger purée
1 large fresh green chilli, de-seeded and chopped
2 teaspoons sunflower oil
1–2 teaspoons medium strength Balti curry powder
2 tablespoons dried split red lentils
1 courgette, chopped
2 tablespoons chopped fresh coriander
salt and freshly ground black pepper

For the pilaff

125 g (4¹/₂ oz) basmati rice
1 bay leaf
¹/₂ stick cinnamon
4 whole cardamoms
¹/₄ teaspoon cumin seeds
¹/₄ teaspoon ground turmeric
salt and freshly ground black pepper

1 In a bowl, mix the desiccated coconut with the boiling water. Set aside for 10 minutes and then strain the liquid. Throw away the coconut and reserve the liquid.
2 Meanwhile, mix together the onion, carrot, celery, garlic purée, ginger purée, chilli and oil in a large saucepan. Heat until the mixture starts to sizzle, and then add 3 tablespoons of water. Cover the pan and cook gently for 5 minutes.
3 Remove the lid from the pan, mix in the curry powder and cook it briefly. Add the lentils, courgette, the reserved coconut water and seasoning.
4 Bring the mixture to the boil, and then cover and simmer for about 10 minutes. Mix in the coriander and check the seasoning.
5 Meanwhile, make the pilaff. Place the rice in a sieve and rinse it under a cold running tap. Put it in a medium size saucepan with 300 ml (½ pint) cold water. Add the bay leaf, spices and seasoning. Bring to the boil, stirring, and then cover and simmer gently for 10 minutes. Do not lift the lid.
6 Allow the rice to stand for 5 minutes, and then separate the grains with a fork. Serve the rice with the curry spooned over.

Top tip There are many varieties of basmati rice, choose a good brand like Tilda for the best fragrance and texture.

Variation The pilaff can be made on its own to serve with other curries or your favourite vegetable stews.

Sicilian Caponata: a lovely, sunny dish full of the flavours of Italy. Served here with 150 g (5½ oz) cooked spaghetti for just 3½ Points.

SICILIAN CAPONATA

3 Points per recipe

Ⓥ *Serves: 2*

Preparation time: 10 minutes

Cooking time: 20 minutes

Calories per serving: 190

Freezing: not recommended

Like a sweet and sour ratatouille, this dish is delicious served hot or cold with 150 g (5½ oz) cooked spaghetti or rice for an extra 2 or 3 Points respectively.

1 medium red onion, sliced thickly

1 large garlic clove, crushed

1 small aubergine, chopped into small cubes

1 medium courgette, chopped into small cubes

1 red pepper, de-seeded and sliced

1 tablespoon olive oil

400 g can of chopped tomatoes

1 tablespoon balsamic or red wine vinegar

1 tablespoon fresh lemon juice

2 teaspoons sugar

1 tablespoon capers

salt and freshly ground black pepper

1 Place the onion, garlic, aubergine, courgette and pepper with the oil and 150 ml (5 fl oz) water in a large saucepan. Heat the mixture until it all starts to sizzle, and then cover and cook on a medium heat for 10 minutes, stirring once or twice.

2 When the vegetables are softened, add the tomatoes, vinegar, lemon juice, sugar and capers. Season and bring to the boil. Reduce the heat and simmer, uncovered, for about 7–8 minutes. Check the seasoning before serving.

TOFU KEBABS WITH PEANUT SAUCE

5 Points per recipe

Ⓥ *Serves: 2*

Preparation time: 15 minutes

Cooking time: 15 minutes

Calories per serving: 220

Freezing: not recommended

Treat yourself to an exotic Thai style main meal, served with a luxurious peanut sauce that is unbelievably low in Points.

200 g pack of tofu, cut into bite size squares

2 tablespoons light soy sauce

1 teaspoon sesame oil

1 large garlic clove, crushed

1 red or yellow pepper, de-seeded, cut into bite size squares

1 Little Gem lettuce, shredded, to serve

For the sauce

1 spring onion, chopped finely

¼ teaspoon chilli powder

½ teaspoon caster sugar

2 teaspoons white wine vinegar

1 tablespoon crunchy peanut butter

1 Mix the tofu together with 1 tablespoon of the soy sauce, the sesame oil and garlic. Leave it to marinate for 5 minutes.

2 Thread the tofu and pepper pieces alternately on to wooden satay sticks.

3 In a small saucepan, place the sauce ingredients together with the remaining soy sauce and heat for 2–3 minutes until just hot and blended together.

4 Preheat the grill to a high heat. Grill the tofu kebabs for about 5–6 minutes, turning them once, until they are crispy. Serve the kebabs on the shredded lettuce with the sauce spooned over.

Tofu Kebabs with Peanut Sauce: only 2½ Points per serving.

Tomato, Courgette and Parmesan Tarts: these melt-in-the mouth tarts are like little pizzas – but for just 5½ Points.

TOMATO, COURGETTE AND PARMESAN TARTS

22½ Points per recipe

(V) Serves: 4

Preparation time: 5 minutes

Cooking time: 25 minutes

Calories per serving: 220

Freezing: not recommended

One bite of these crispy tarts with their blend of tomato, courgette and Parmesan cheese whisks you off to the shores of the Mediterranean! Accompany them with a tossed mixed salad for a perfect summer lunch.

---

1 sheet ready rolled puff pastry

1 large courgette, cut into slices 5 mm (¼ inch) thick

1 teaspoon olive oil

---

4 medium tomatoes, sliced thinly

25 g (1 oz) freshly grated Parmesan cheese

salt and freshly ground black pepper

---

1 Preheat the oven to Gas Mark 7/220°C/fan oven 200°C. Using a 10 cm (4 inch) saucer as a template, cut out four discs of pastry and place them on a heavy non stick baking sheet. Prick the pastry well.

2 Place another heavy non stick baking sheet on top and bake for 12–15 minutes until the pastry discs are pale golden, crisp and flat. Remove the top baking sheet.

3 Meanwhile, preheat the grill. Brush one side of the courgette slices with the oil. Arrange them on a baking sheet, oiled side up, and grill them under a high heat for about 5 minutes just on one side, until they are softened.

4 Lay the courgette slices on the four pastry discs. Place the tomato slices on top, arranged so the slices overlap each other. You can pile the slices high because they shrink while cooking. Season well with salt and pepper, and sprinkle over the Parmesan.

5 Return the tarts to the oven for another 5 minutes or so, until the cheese just melts. Cool slightly before serving.

Variation You can make these tarts even lower in Points by substituting 4 wholemeal bread slices, lightly toasted, for the pastry discs. The Points will be 2 per serving.

EGG CURRY

11½ Points per recipe

(V) Serves: 2

Preparation time: 10 minutes

Cooking time: 20 minutes

Calories per serving: 415

Freezing: not recommended

Lightly spicy and aromatic, this is a simple curry with a tangy touch. Serve this as a main meal with chopped fresh tomatoes.

---

2 large eggs

100 g (3½ oz) long grain rice

1 tablespoon chopped fresh parsley or coriander

1 teaspoon poppy seeds

1 onion, sliced

1 large garlic clove, crushed

1 tablespoon ginger purée

1 large fresh green chilli

---

1 teaspoon sunflower oil

1 teaspoon mild or medium curry powder

200 g can of chopped tomatoes

150 g tub of low fat plain bio yogurt

1 teaspoon plain white flour

salt and freshly ground black pepper

2 tablespoons coarsely grated carrot, to serve

---

1 Hard boil the eggs for 8 minutes, and then cool them under cold running water. Peel and cut them into quarters. Set aside.

2 At the same time as cooking the eggs, boil the rice in lightly salted, boiling water according to the pack instructions. Drain the rice, and then mix in the parsley or coriander and poppy seeds. Keep this rice mixture warm.

3 Put the onion, garlic, ginger purée, chilli and oil with 3 tablespoons of water in a medium size saucepan and heat until the mixture sizzles. Sauté gently for 5 minutes and then mix in the curry powder and cook for 1 minute.

4 Stir in the chopped tomatoes, 100 ml (3½ fl oz) of water and seasoning. Add the egg quarters to the pan. Simmer for 5 minutes.

5 Blend together the yogurt and flour and stir this mixture into the pan. Heat through, but do not boil. Check the seasoning. Divide the rice mixture between two serving plates and then spoon on the egg curry. Sprinkle over the grated carrot and serve.

Top tip Coarsely grated carrot makes a colourful and healthy garnish if you have no fresh herbs for chopping.

Variation Substitute 100 g (3½ oz) of Quorn pieces for the egg. The Points are 4½ per serving.

Chocolate Roulade
with Creamy
Raspberry Crush:
a heavenly dessert
for just 4 Points.

puddings

The puddings in this chapter range from the light and fruity to the rich and indulgent, but they all have two things in common – they all taste divine and are wonderfully low in Points! The great thing is they can all be prepared in 30 minutes or under, so when you fancy a sweet treat – from something fruity to something with chocolate – you'll find plenty to tuck into in double quick time!

CHOCOLATE ROULADE WITH CREAMY RASPBERRY CRUSH

(4 POINTS)

17 Points per recipe

ⓥ Serves: 4

*Preparation and cooking time:
20 minutes + 5 minutes cooling
Calories per serving: 285
Freezing: not recommended*

This rich and creamy roulade has an intense chocolate flavour which contrasts perfectly with the delicious tang of raspberries. This is a quick and impressive dessert, great if friends drop around for supper.

2 large eggs
80 g (3 oz) caster sugar
75 g (2¾ oz) plain white flour
2 tablespoons cocoa powder
a good pinch of salt
200 g (7 oz) fresh raspberries
200 g (7 oz) quark
1 tablespoon clear honey (optional)
1 teaspoon of icing sugar, for dusting

1 Heat the oven to Gas Mark 6/200°C/ fan oven 180°C. Line a Swiss roll tin, about 30 cm × 23 cm (12 inches × 9 inches) with non stick baking parchment.

2 Put the eggs and sugar in a large heatproof bowl, and place the bowl over a saucepan of simmering water. Using a hand held electric whisk (see Top tip), beat the mixture steadily until you have a thick, yellow foam – it should leave a trail when you lift out the whisk. Remove the bowl from the pan and let it cool.

3 Sift together the flour, cocoa powder and salt. Gently fold these dry ingredients into the eggy foam. Now spread the mixture into the prepared tin.

4 Bake in the oven for 8–10 minutes until the sponge is firm to the touch. Remove the tin from the oven and let it cool for 5 minutes. Turn the sponge out on to a wire rack and carefully peel off the lining paper.

5 Trim off the crusty edges of the sponge and cover it with a fresh sheet of non stick baking parchment. Roll up the sponge, enclosing the parchment, and allow it to cool.

6 Meanwhile, place the raspberries in a bowl and crush them with a fork. Stir in the quark. Sweeten the mixture with the honey, if using.

7 Unroll the sponge and remove the baking parchment. Spread it with the raspberry cream and then re-roll it. Place the roulade on a platter and sift over the icing sugar.

Top tip Electric whisks are best for whisking eggs to a thick foam. You can buy small hand held ones at very reasonable prices. Alternatively if you have an electric mixer with a whisk attachment, then you can use that without beating over a pan of simmering water.

Banana and Chocolate Fool: a delicious pud that can be put together in a few minutes – and only 2 Points!

BANANA AND CHOCOLATE FOOL

7 Points per recipe

Ⓥ Serves: 4

Preparation time: 12 minutes

Calories per serving: 120

Freezing: not recommended

This rich tasting pudding is an excellent way to use up bananas that are past their best.

2 large ripe bananas
juice of 1 small lemon
2 teaspoons artificial sweetener or to taste (optional)
200 g tub of very low fat plain fromage frais
20 g (³/₄ oz) dark chocolate, grated finely

1 Blend the bananas in a food processor with the lemon juice and sweetener, if using.

2 Transfer the banana mixture to a mixing bowl and fold in the fromage frais.

3 Divide the mixture between four sundae or ramekin dishes. Sprinkle over the grated chocolate and chill the fools in the refrigerator until firm.

HOT TOFFEE APPLES

9 Points per recipe

Ⓥ Serves: 4

Preparation and cooking time: 15 minutes

Calories per serving: 135

Freezing: not recommended

Give in to temptation with this wonderfully tasty and sticky low Point pudding.

3 tablespoons toffee flavoured ice cream syrup
2 large, unpeeled dessert apples, sliced thinly
500 g tub of fruit flavoured low fat yogurt (e.g. strawberry flavoured)

1 Heat the toffee syrup in a frying pan and toss in the apple slices. Cook for 3 minutes, stirring gently.

2 Divide the yogurt between four serving bowls and spoon the hot apples on top to serve.

Variations This is also good with bananas or pears. The Points will remain the same.

Try using natural maple syrup instead of toffee ice cream syrup – delicious! The Points remain the same.

FRUITS OF THE FOREST CREAM

4 Points per recipe

Ⓥ Serves: 4

Preparation time: 12 minutes

Calories per serving: 80

Freezing: not recommended

This creamy, fruity dish is full of the flavours of summer.

250 g pack of ripe strawberries, hulled
125 g (4¹/₂ oz) blueberries or blackberries
125 g (4¹/₂ oz) raspberries
200 g tub of quark
1 tablespoon artificial sweetener or to taste
4 mint sprigs for decoration

1 In a big bowl, crush the strawberries with the other fruits using a fork or the back of a ladle. Reserve 4 teaspoons of crushed fruit for decoration.

2 Add the quark and stir until smooth. Add the sweetener to taste.

3 Spoon the mixture into four serving bowls and top with the reserved crushed fruit and the mint.

Variation Try using very low fat fromage frais instead of quark and add a little grated lemon zest. The Points will remain the same.

Fruits of the Forest Cream: who can resist such a divine-tasting dessert? All that creamy, fruity flavour for just 1 Point.

Hot Spiced Fruit Salad: fruit with a twist! Just 2½ Points.

HOT SPICED FRUIT SALAD

9½ Points per recipe

Ⓥ ⓥₑ *Serves: 4*
Preparation time: 10 minutes
Cooking time: 15 minutes
Calories per serving: 160
Freezing: recommended

Fruit salads are just as good served hot. Dried fruits soaked in rum and spice mix well with autumnal fruits such as apples, pears and plums. Serve this salad warm for the best flavour.

---

227 g can of apricots in natural juice

2 tablespoons rum

1 teaspoon mixed spice or ½ teaspoon ground cinnamon

75 g (2¾ oz) dried cranberries

50 g (1¾ oz) raisins

1 large, unpeeled dessert apple (e.g Cox or Braeburn), cored and sliced

1 large, unpeeled dessert pear, cored and sliced

2 ripe red plums, de-stoned and sliced

---

1 Put the apricots and their juice in a medium size saucepan with the rum and mixed spice or cinnamon and heat for 2 minutes. Mix in the dried fruits and set aside.

2 Mix the fresh fruits into the hot dried fruit mixture and spoon the fruit salad into four serving dishes.

Variation You can omit the rum if you like and add a teaspoon of vanilla essence instead. The Points will be 2 per serving.

PEAR BELLE HELENE

9 Points per recipe

Ⓥ *Serves: 4*
Preparation and cooking time: 10 minutes
Calories per serving: 140
Freezing: not recommended

This is a quick, low Point version of the great classic. Absolutely divine! The pear can be peeled or unpeeled, just as you prefer.

---

420 g can of low fat rice pudding

1 large ripe Conference or Comice pear, chopped into bite size pieces

For the sauce

4 tablespoons cold water

1 teaspoon caster sugar

1 tablespoon cocoa powder

2 tablespoons single cream

---

1 Make the sauce first. Put the water, sugar and cocoa powder in a small saucepan. Bring the pan to the boil, stirring continuously, until you have a smooth, thick sauce. Reduce the heat and simmer for 1 minute. Remove the pan from the heat and stir in the cream. Allow the sauce to cool, stirring from time to time.

2 Divide the rice pudding between four sundae dishes. Place the chopped pear on top of the rice pudding.

3 Spoon the sauce over each one and serve.

Top tips Single cream is surprisingly lower in Points than some reduced fat creams and cheeses – as long as it is used in small quantities.

This sauce is brilliant poured over bananas or low fat ice cream. Remember to adjust the Points accordingly.

RASPBERRY AND MELON CRUSH

3½ Points per recipe

Ⓥ ⓥₑ *Serves: 4*
Preparation time: 20 minutes
Calories per serving: 55
Freezing: not recommended

This luscious dessert is so easy to prepare and so refreshing. Wonderful on a summer's evening.

---

250 g pack of frozen raspberries

half a ripe honeydew melon

---

1 Tip the raspberries into a food processor and leave them for about 15 minutes, until they start to thaw but remain half frozen.

2 Meanwhile, scoop out the seeds from the melon. Peel it and cut it into chunks. Add the melon to the food processor and blend with the raspberries until the fruit becomes slushy.

3 Spoon the crush into glasses or individual bowls and serve immediately.

THAI RICE PUDDING

3½ POINTS

14 Points per recipe

Ⓥ Serves: 4
Preparation time: 15 minutes
Cooking time: 15 minutes
Calories per serving: 225
Freezing: not recommended

Thai rice makes a deliciously fragrant, easy to cook rice pudding in under 30 minutes! The mangoes complement the flavour of this dish perfectly.

2 tablespoons desiccated coconut
750 ml (1¹/₃ pint) skimmed milk
100 g (3¹/₂ oz) jasmine rice
granulated artificial sweetener, to taste
1 fresh lemon grass stem (optional)
1 medium ripe mango, peeled and sliced thinly

1 In a medium size saucepan, heat the coconut and the milk until boiling. Remove the pan from the heat and cool for 15 minutes.
2 Strain the milk mixture and then discard the coconut.
3 Meanwhile, place the rice in enough boiling water just to cover it and blanch it for 2 minutes. Drain, return the rice to the pan and add the coconut flavoured milk and sweetener.
4 With a sharp knife, slash the lemon grass stem, if using, and add it to the rice. Bring the pan to the boil, and then reduce the heat and simmer for about 15 minutes, stirring occasionally.
5 When the rice has swollen and softened and the mixture has thickened, remove the lemon grass and allow the rice to cool.
6 Serve the rice pudding in small dishes topped with mango slices.

Top tip Instead of using high fat coconut cream in recipes, make your own lower fat coconut milk by heating desiccated coconut in skimmed milk.

Variation This is equally good with fragrant basmati rice instead of jasmine rice, however don't use the easy cook variety – it won't give you the same soft creaminess. The Points will remain the same.

ORANGE, STRAWBERRY AND PINK GRAPEFRUIT SALAD

1 POINT

4½ Points per recipe

Ⓥ Ⓥg Serves: 4
Preparation time: 15 minutes
Calories per serving: 85
Freezing: not recommended

The pretty colours of the fruits make this refreshing dessert very attractive. It's ideal for entertaining. Serve it in large wine glasses or delicate sundae dishes.

2 large seedless oranges
1 large pink grapefruit
1 tablespoon clear honey
250 g (9 oz) fresh strawberries, hulled
1 tablespoon roughly chopped fresh mint, to decorate

1 Using a serrated knife, cut the tops and bases from the oranges and grapefruit. Cut off the skin and membrane of each one in downward strokes, leaving the peeled fruit whole. Now cut the fruit into halves lengthways and then into slices.
2 Mix the honey with the orange and grapefruit slices.
3 Cut the strawberries into quarters. Gently mix them in with the citrus fruits and spoon it all into four wine or sundae glasses to serve. Top with a sprinkling of mint. Chill lightly until required.

Variations Try fresh raspberries instead of strawberries. The Points remain the same.

CARAMELISED PINEAPPLE

6½ Points per recipe

Ⓥ Ⓥⓔ *Serves: 4*

Preparation and cooking time:
15 minutes + 10 minutes cooling
Calories per serving: 85
Freezing: not recommended

These pineapple slices have a
caramelised toffee flavour, giving
them a wonderfully indulgent feel.

1 medium ripe pineapple

2 tablespoons clear honey

ground cinnamon, to taste

150 g pot of low fat plain bio yogurt,
to serve

1 Cut the top from the pineapple,
then using a sharp knife, cut off the
skin. Use a small potato peeler to
dig out any 'eyes'.

2 Cut the pineapple into eight slices,
and then using a small scone cutter
cut out the core – although some
people like to eat the core!

3 Preheat the grill to a high heat and
line the grill pan with foil. Arrange
the pineapple in a single layer on
the foil. In a cup, heat the honey
for a few seconds in the microwave
and then brush it over the pineapple
rings.

4 Sprinkle the pineapple slices with
cinnamon to taste, and then grill
them on one side only until they are
golden brown and bubbling.

5 Tip the pineapple slices into a
shallow bowl to allow the flavours to
blend together. Allow them to cool
slightly for 10 minutes, and then
serve the slices warm with the yogurt.

Top tip Fresh pineapples make good
value, quick desserts, but you will
need a sharp knife to peel them.
Check they are ripe by pulling out
a leaf at the crown. If it comes out
easily, the fruit is juicy and naturally
sweet.

Variation This is equally delicious
with halved and stoned fresh
peaches. Use one peach per person.
The Points will remain the same.

FILO CUPS WITH APRICOT CREAM

Ⓟ **2 POINTS**

9 Points per recipe

Ⓥ *Serves: 4*

Preparation time: 15 minutes
Cooking time: 12 minutes
Calories per serving: 140
Freezing: not recommended

These little pastries are heavenly –
the melt-in-the-mouth filo pastry
contrasting perfectly with the tangy
creamy filling…delicious!

1 teaspoon icing sugar

2 tablespoons low fat spread, melted

4 × 30 cm × 17 cm (12 inch × 6½ inch)
sheets filo pastry

420 g can of apricots in natural juice,
drained

200 g (7 oz) very low fat plain
fromage frais

artificial sweetener (optional)

ground cinnamon, to serve

1 Mix the icing sugar with the
melted low fat spread. With a pastry
brush, dab this mixture over each
filo sheet, and then cut each one into
quarters. Layer the quartered sheets
into four bun tins, placing them at
angles to each other to form the cups.

2 Heat the oven to Gas Mark 5/
190°C/fan oven 170°C. Bake the filo
cups for 10–12 minutes until they are
golden brown and crisp. Cool them
until required.

3 Pat the apricots dry with kitchen
paper and then chop them finely.
Mix the apricot pieces with the
fromage frais   add sweetener to the
mixture if you like. Chill the apricot
cream until ready to serve.

4 Spoon the apricot cream into the
cups, dust with cinnamon and serve.

Variation Try a 400 g (14 oz) punnet
of fresh ripe strawberries instead of
apricots. Crush with a fork until
mushy but not too runny. Omit the
cinnamon but stir ½ teaspoon vanilla
essence into the fromage frais. The
Points will remain the same.

QUICK FRUIT CRUMBLE 4 POINTS

15¹/₂ Points per recipe

v *Serves:* 4

Preparation time: 10 minutes

Cooking time: 20 minutes

Calories per serving: 240

Freezing: recommended

This simple and satisfying dessert is assembled in no time using a can of fruit and a quickly whizzed up crumble topping – just right for a mid week pudding. Serve this with low fat natural yogurt or low fat custard, adding the extra Points.

420 g can of peaches in natural juice, drained

1 large ripe banana, sliced thinly

50 g (1³/₄ oz) low fat spread

100 g (3¹/₂ oz) plain white flour

1 tablespoon light soft brown sugar

2 tablespoons porridge oats

freshly grated nutmeg

1 Preheat the oven to Gas Mark 5/ 190°C/fan oven 170°C.

2 Tip the canned fruit into a medium size baking dish – chop the fruit if necessary. Mix in the banana slices.

3 Place the low fat spread, flour and sugar in a food processor and whiz until the mixture resembles fine breadcrumbs. Stir in the porridge oats. Spoon this topping over the fruit and sprinkle over nutmeg.

4 Place the dish on a baking tray and bake in the oven for 20 minutes until the topping is lightly browned.

Variation In spring try 400 g (14 oz) tender, pink forced rhubarb instead of the peaches. There's no need to precook it. Chop it and add 1 tablespoon caster sugar. The Points are 3¹/₂ per serving.

Pear Brulées: no dessert lover could resist this 2 Point pud.

PEAR BRULEES 2 POINTS

9 Points per recipe

v *Serves:* 4

Preparation and cooking time: 15 minutes

Calories per serving: 130

Freezing: not recommended

These fruit brulées are a low Point version of this favourite dessert.

1 large ripe pear (e.g. Comice, Conference), chopped

200 g tub of quark

140 g tub of flavoured low fat yogurt (e.g. lemon or vanilla)

4 tablespoons demerara sugar

1 Preheat the grill. Divide the pear between four heatproof ramekins.

2 Beat together the quark and yogurt until smooth and spoon the mixture on top of the pears. Sprinkle the tops evenly with the sugar.

3 Place the dishes under a very hot grill to caramelise the sugar until it dissolves. If you have a cook's blow torch you can flame the sugar with that.

4 Cool the brulées for 5 minutes before serving.

Variation All sorts of fruits could be used instead of pears. Try raspberries, sliced peaches, strawberries or plums, remembering to alter the Points accordingly.

Quick Fruit Crumble: a 4 Point version of the family favourite.

Chocolate Scones:
delicious filled
with creamy
fromage frais
and jam and for
just 2 Points!

cakes
& bakes

In this chapter you will find some delicious low Point recipes, from quick homemade bread that will smell divine as it cooks, to fantastic tray bakes. Whatever you fancy there will be something here you'll love. There's even wonderful dark and rich chocolate scones (below) – ideal for tea on a chilly afternoon.

CHOCOLATE SCONES

12¹/₂ Points per recipe

V *Makes: 6 scones*
Preparation time: 10 minutes
Cooking time: 12 minutes
Calories per scone: 140
Freezing: not recommended

Fresh baked scones hot from the oven are one of the nicest sweet treats – especially when they have a delicious chocolate flavour. The raspberry jam and creamy fromage frais filling will make them seem really indulgent, yet they are unbelievably low in Points.

100 g (3¹/₂ oz) self raising white flour plus 2 teaspoons for dusting
15 g (¹/₂ oz) cocoa powder
a good pinch of salt
¹/₂ teaspoon baking powder
1 tablespoon caster sugar
¹/₂ teaspoon vanilla extract
20 g (³/₄ oz) low fat spread
about 3–4 tablespoons skimmed milk
200 g tub of very low fat fromage frais
100 g (3¹/₂ oz) reduced sugar raspberry jam

1 Heat the oven to Gas Mark 6/ 200°C/fan oven 180°C. Sift the flour, cocoa powder, salt and baking powder into a food processor. Add the sugar, vanilla extract and low fat spread and process until the mixture resembles fine breadcrumbs.
2 Tip the mixture into a mixing bowl. Using a table knife, mix in

the milk, adding spoonfuls until you have a firm but soft dough. You may not need all the milk and the dough should not be sticky.
3 Turn out the dough on to a lightly floured board and knead it lightly until smooth. Pat it out to a 1.5 cm (⁵/₈ inch) thickness and cut it into six 5 cm (2 inch) rounds, re-kneading any leftover dough.
4 Place the rounds on a non stick baking tray or on a tray lined with non stick baking parchment. Bake for 12 minutes until risen and the sides bounce back when pinched.
5 Cool slightly and then halve them and fill with the fromage frais and jam. Top with more fromage frais and jam.

Top tip You don't have to cut scones in rounds. To save time, simply shape the dough into a round or square and cut it into six wedges or smaller squares.

At just 1 Point each, these Lemon and Vanilla Fingers are a treat you can afford!

LEMON AND VANILLA FINGERS

1 POINT

12½ Points per recipe

(V) *Makes: 12 fingers*
Preparation time: 15 minutes
Cooking time: 10 minutes
Calories per finger: 70
Freezing: not recommended

You'll find these delicious fingers very versatile. Simply nibble them on their own or serve them with fruit salads or iced desserts, remembering to add the extra Points.

2 large eggs
85 g (3 oz) caster sugar
1 teaspoon vanilla extract
finely grated zest of 1 lemon
85 g (3 oz) plain white flour, sifted

1 Grease and line a large, heavy metal baking sheet with non stick baking parchment. Heat the oven to Gas Mark 6/200°C/fan oven 180°C.
2 Bring a medium size saucepan, half filled with water, to a gentle boil. Put the eggs, sugar and vanilla extract into a large heatproof bowl and place the bowl over the pan of water. Using an electric hand held whisk (or balloon whisk if you have to beat by hand) beat as fast as possible until you have a firm, pale golden foam – the mixture should leave a trail when you lift out the beaters.
3 Remove the bowl from the heat and continue whisking for 2–3 minutes and then gently fold in the lemon zest and flour using a large metal spoon.
4 Fit a plain 1.5 cm (⅝ inch) nozzle into a piping bag. Put the bag into a tall jug and roll down the top. Spoon the mixture into the piping bag.
5 Twist the top to seal the bag with one hand and holding the nozzle in the other hand, pipe 12 straight lengths about 10 cm (4 inches) long on to the baking sheet. If you don't own a piping bag, spoon mounds of the mixture, flattening them with the back of a teaspoon to make 12 rounds about 3 cm (1¼ inches) in diameter.
6 Bake for 5–7 minutes until the biscuits are pale golden and firm. Cool for 2 minutes, and then lift the fingers off the baking sheet with a palette knife on to a wire tray. Let them cool completely.

Top tip Eggs used for baking should be at room temperature. That way they whisk to a better volume. If you store eggs in the fridge remove them 30 minutes before use.

CARROT CUP CAKES

2½ POINTS

21 Points per recipe

(V) *Makes: 9 cakes*
Preparation time: 12 minutes
Cooking time: 17 minutes
Calories per cake: 145
Freezing: not recommended

Carrot cake is one of the great delicious cake mixtures of all time. Grated carrot and ripe bananas add moistness, which enables you to cut down on Points without losing any of the flavour.

100 g (3½ oz) self raising white flour
1 teaspoon baking powder
½ teaspoon ground cinnamon
50 g (1¾ oz) polyunsaturated margarine
100 g (3½ oz) soft brown sugar
1 teaspoon vanilla extract
1 egg
2 tablespoons skimmed milk
1 small ripe banana, chopped roughly
1 medium carrot, grated coarsely
1 teaspoon icing sugar, for dusting

1 Preheat the oven to Gas Mark 5/190°C/fan oven 170°C. Line a bun tin with nine paper baking cases.
2 Put the flour, baking powder, cinnamon, margarine, sugar, vanilla extract, egg, milk and banana in a food processor and blend until smooth, scraping down the sides once or twice.
3 Mix in the carrot, blending it in with short pulses of the food processor until just incorporated.
4 Spoon the mixture into the paper cases and bake for about 15–17 minutes until firm and springy on top.
5 Place the cakes on a wire rack and dust the tops with icing sugar.

Carrot Cup Cakes: these delicious 2½ Point cakes are perfect with a mid-morning cup of coffee.

Apricot and Cranberry Squares: at just 2 Points each, these are perfect for those hungry moments.

APRICOT AND CRANBERRY SQUARES

2 POINTS

24½ Points per recipe

ⓥ Makes: 12 squares
Preparation time: 10 minutes
Cooking time: 17 minutes
Calories per square: 135
Freezing: recommended

These delicious fruity squares use a purée of apricots to make them moist and luscious. They taste wonderful served with a mug of steaming hot tea.

---

400 g can of apricots in juice, drained
250 g (9 oz) self raising white flour
1 teaspoon baking powder
1 teaspoon ground mixed spice or cinnamon
2 tablespoons sunflower oil
50 g (1¾ oz) dark soft brown sugar
4 tablespoons skimmed milk
1 large egg, beaten
3 tablespoons dried cranberries

---

1 Preheat the oven to Gas Mark 5/ 190°C/fan oven 170°C. Line the base of a non stick Swiss roll tin with non stick baking parchment.
2 Purée the apricots in a food processor.
3 Put the flour, baking powder and spice into a large bowl and mix well with a wooden spoon.

4 Add the oil, sugar, milk, egg and apricot purée and beat well. Stir in the cranberries.
5 Spoon the mixture into the prepared tin. Level the surface and bake for about 17 minutes until the top feels springy.
6 Cut the cake into 12 squares while still in the tin, and then turn out on to a wire rack and peel off the baking parchment.

Top tip These squares are perfect for the odd hungry moment. Spread them out on a wire tray and freeze solid. Tip into a plastic bag and store in the freezer. Thaw one at a time when needed!

Variation Use 400 g canned prunes in juice instead of the apricots. Be sure to stone them before putting them in the food processor. The Points will remain the same.

OATMEAL BISCUITS

1 POINT

13½ Points per recipe

ⓥ Makes: 12 biscuits
Preparation time: 10 minutes
Cooking time: 15 minutes
Calories per biscuit: 70
Freezing: recommended

Make a batch of these delicious, crunchy biscuits and freeze them, then just remove one when you want a snack, allowing a little defrosting time.

---

50 g (1¾ oz) plain white flour plus 2 teaspoons for dusting
a good pinch of bicarbonate of soda

100 g (3½ oz) oatmeal
2 teaspoons light soft brown sugar (optional)
25 g (1 oz) raisins (optional)
25 g (1 oz) polyunsaturated margarine
5 tablespoons hot water

---

1 Heat the oven to Gas Mark 7/ 220°C/fan oven 200°C. Sift together the flour, bicarbonate of soda, oatmeal and sugar, if using. Stir in the raisins, if using.
2 Mix together the margarine and hot water, stirring until the margarine has melted. Beat this mixture into the dry ingredients to make a firm, but not dry dough. If necessary, add extra dribbles of hot water.

3 Turn out the dough on to a wooden board dusted with a little flour. Roll out to ½ cm (¼ inch) thickness. Cut the dough into neat squares, measuring about 5 cm (2 inches).
4 Line a heavy baking sheet with non stick baking parchment and place the oatmeal biscuits on top. Prick each one 2 or 3 times with a fork. Bake in the oven for 15 minutes until firm, and then transfer to a wire tray to cool completely.

Top tip You need old fashioned oatmeal for these biscuits to give them a lovely crisp texture. Most supermarkets stock it these days, or try the health food shops.

ROSEMARY SODA BREAD

 5½ POINTS

22 Points per recipe

Ⓥ Serves: 4

Preparation time: 10 minutes

Cooking time: 20 minutes

Calories per serving: 355

Freezing: not recommended

This delicious, aromatic bread tastes as good as it smells. Serve it warm with soup for a lunchtime treat.

200 g (7 oz) plain white flour
200 g (7 oz) wholemeal flour
1½ teaspoons bicarbonate of soda
1½ teaspoons baking powder
1 tablespoon olive oil spread
1½ teaspoons dried rosemary, chopped finely
½ teaspoon fine sea salt
freshly ground black pepper
250 ml (9 fl oz) skimmed milk

1 Preheat the oven to Gas Mark 7/ 220°C/fan oven 200°C.

2 Put the flours, bicarbonate of soda, baking powder, olive oil spread, rosemary, salt and pepper in a food processor, and blend for about 20 seconds.

3 Tip the mixture into a bowl and gradually mix in the skimmed milk using a table knife to make a firm, but not too dry, dough. Knead lightly until the dough is smooth.

4 Cover a baking sheet with non stick baking parchment. Shape the dough into a flat round about 20 cm (8 inches) in diameter. With a sharp knife, score a deep cross on top to mark it into four.

5 Bake for about 20 minutes until the bread has risen and is springy to the touch. You can check it is cooked by knocking the underneath – if it sounds hollow, it is ready.

BREAKFAST PANCAKES

1 POINT

10½ Points per recipe

Ⓥ Makes: 12 pancakes

Preparation time: 10 minutes

Cooking time: 15 minutes

Calories per pancake: 55

Freezing: not recommended

These are especially nice served for a leisurely breakfast or brunch.

75 g (2¾ oz) plain white flour
25 g (1 oz) wholemeal flour
½ teaspoon baking powder
1 egg
1 tablespoon clear honey
300 ml (½ pint) skimmed milk
3 tablespoons cooked brown rice (optional)
low fat cooking spray

1 Put the flours, baking powder, egg, honey and skimmed milk in a large bowl and beat well until smooth. Mix in the rice, if using.

2 Spray a heavy based, non stick frying pan with low fat cooking spray and heat it. When the pan is hot, drop in heaped tablespoons of the pancake mixture, 3–4 at a time and cook until the top almost sets and bubbles start to rise.

3 Flip the pancakes over and cook the other side briefly. Repeat the cooking process with the remaining batter.

This Rosemary Soda Bread is delicately herby and so quick to do! 5½ Points per serving.